# Western Civilization
## *Renaissance to Modern Times*

Fr. Peter Samuel Kucer, MSA

En Route Books & Media, LLC
St. Louis, MO, USA

En Route Books and Media, LLC
5705 Rhodes Avenue
St. Louis, MO 63109

Cover credit: TJ Burdick

Library of Congress Control Number: 2017956389

Copyright © 2021 Peter Samuel Kucer

ISBN-10:0-9994704-4-2
ISBN-13: 978-0-9994704-4-2

No part of this booklet may be reproduced, stored in a retrieval system, or transmitted in any form, or by any means, electronic, mechanical, photocopying, or otherwise, without the prior written permission of the author.

# DEDICATION

In memory of my mother, Roberta Kucer, who instilled in me a love of study and a love of her people, the chosen people.

In addition, I dedicate this book to the members of my community, the Missionaries of the Holy Apostles.

# ACKNOWLEDGMENTS

I would particularly like to acknowledge Bishop Isaac Martinez, MSA, former General of the Missionaries of the Holy Apostles, who gave me permission to publish, and Bishop Christian Rodembourg, MSA, who as the first MSA to be ordained a bishop brought our MSA charism into a deeper ecclesial dimension. Special thanks to Dr. Sebastian Mahfood, OP, president of En Route Books and Media, for publishing this work.

# CONTENTS

Chapter 1 Monarchies: Limited and Checked or Supreme? 1
   British Monarchy and Parliament ........................2
   French Monarchy and Absolutism ......................10
   Baroque Art .......................................................144
      Gianlorenzo Bernini (1598-1680)...................144
      Michelangelo Merisi da Caravaggio (1571-1610)......177
      Artemisia Gentileschi (1593-1656)................188
      Diego Velázquez (1599-1660) .......................20
      Rococo or Late Baroque - Jean-Honoré Fragonard (1732-1806) ..............................................21
   Quiz 1 for Chapter 1 ..........................................22
Chapter 2 The Rise of Western Science........................25
   Rationalism and Empiricism ...............................26
      Rene Descartes (1596-1650) .........................26
      Francis Bacon (1561-1626)............................27
   Promoters of the Scientific Method....................28
      Nicholas Copernicus (1473-1543) .................28
      Tycho Brahe (1546-1601) .............................34
      Johannes Kepler (1571-1630) and Galileo Galilei (1564-1642) ..............................................35
      Isaac Newton (1642-1727).............................37
      William Harvey (1578-1657)..........................39
   Neo-Classical Art ................................................41

Jacques-Louis David (1748-1825)...........41
Antonio Canova (1757-1822) ...........43
Benjamin Latrobe (1764-1820) ...........44
Quiz 2 for Chapter 2 ...........46
Chapter 3 Politics and Revolutions...........49
American Revolution...........49
John Locke (1632-1704)...........53
Montesquieu (1689-1755) ...........56
Philosophy of the French Revolution...........57
The Four Governments of the French Revolution ...........61
1. The National Constituent Assembly (1789-1791)..61
2. The Legislative Assembly (1791-1792) ...........65
3. The National Convention (1792-1795)...........67
4. The Directory (1795-1799)...........70
Romanticism...........71
J. M. W. Turner, (1775 –1851)...........74
John Constable...........76
Thomas Gainsborough (1727-1788) ...........76
Caspar David Friedrich (1774-1840)...........78
Thomas Cole (1801-1848) ...........79
Albert Bierstadt (1830 –1902) ...........80
Frederic Edwin Church (1826-1900) ...........81
Anne-Louis Trioson (1767-1824)...........82
Henry Fuseli (1741-1824)...........83
William Blake (1757-1827)...........83
Francisco Goya (1746 –1828)...........85
Théodore Géricault (1791-1824) ...........86

## Table of Contents

  Ferdinand Victor Eugène Delacroix (1798-1863) ...... 88
 Quiz 3 for Chapter 3 .................................................................. 89
Chapter 4 The Rise of Nationalistic Ambitions ................... 91
 Napoleon's Nationalistic Ambitions ............................... 92
 German Patriotism and Empire Building ...................... 97
 Italian Nationalism ............................................................. 100
 Austria and Metternich's Anti-Nationalism ................. 105
 Impressionism ..................................................................... 109
  Claude Monet (1840-1926) ......................................... 110
  Édouard Manet (1832-1883) ...................................... 112
  Camille Pissarro (1830-1903) .................................... 113
  Pierre-Auguste Renoir (1841-1919) ......................... 114
  Edgar Degas (1834-1917) ............................................ 116
  Vincent Van Gogh (1853-1890) ................................. 117
  Paul Gauguin (1848-1903) .......................................... 120
  Paul Cézanne (1839-1906) .......................................... 121
  Georges Seurat (1859-1891) ...................................... 123
 Quiz 4 for Chapter 4 ............................................................ 124
Chapter 5 The Industrial Revolution .................................... 127
 Innovations of the Industrial Revolution ..................... 128
 Causes of the Industrial Revolution ............................... 131
 Workers of the Industrial Revolution ............................ 134
 Competing Ideologies of the Industrial Revolution ..... 142
  Mercantilism .................................................................. 142
  Laissez Faire Capitalism or Economic Liberalism.... 144
  Socialism ......................................................................... 145

- Realism .................................................................. 146
  - Gustave Courbet ............................................... 147
  - Jean-François Millet .......................................... 150
  - Honoré Daumier ................................................ 153
  - Winslow Homer ................................................. 156
  - Wilhelm Leibl ................................................... 157
- Symbolism ............................................................ 158
  - Carlos Schwabe ................................................. 158
  - Fernand Khnopff ............................................... 159
  - Viktor M. Vasnetsov .......................................... 160
- Quiz 5 for Chapter 5 ............................................. 160

# Chapter 6 Imperialism and World War I .............. 163
- Imperialism ........................................................... 164
- The Conquest of Africa ........................................ 165
- China and the Opium Wars ................................. 168
- Imperialist Japan .................................................. 170
- World War I (1914-1918) ..................................... 173
- Early Twentieth Century Art ................................ 176
  - Expressionism ................................................... 177
  - Edvard Munch ................................................... 178
  - Franz Marc ........................................................ 179
  - Fauvism ............................................................. 179
  - Henri Matisse .................................................... 180
  - Die Brücke ........................................................ 181
  - Ernst Ludwig Kirchner ...................................... 182
  - Emile Nolde ...................................................... 183
  - Abstraction ........................................................ 183

  Cubism .................................................................... 184
  Georges Braque ..................................................... 184
  Pablo Picasso ........................................................ 185
  Futurism ................................................................ 186
  Umberto Boccioni ................................................ 186
  Angelo de Giudici ................................................ 187
  Dada ..................................................................... 187
  Marcel Duchamp .................................................. 188
  De Stijl .................................................................. 189
  Piet Mondrian ....................................................... 189
 Quiz 6 for Chapter 6 .................................................... 191
Chapter 7 Between World Wars and the Rise of
 Totalitarianism ............................................................. 195
 German Totalitarianism................................................ 195
 Italian Totalitarianism................................................... 207
 Russian Totalitarianism ............................................... 209
 Art of the Inter-War Period.......................................... 211
  Surrealism ............................................................. 211
 Quiz 7 for Chapter 7 .................................................... 213
Chapter 8 World War II ..................................................... 215
 League of Nations ....................................................... 216
 Policy of Appeasement ............................................... 218
 World War II ................................................................. 221
 Nazi and Soviet Propaganda....................................... 224
 Quiz 8 for Chapter 8 .................................................... 229
Chapter 9 Radical Scientific Discoveries ......................... 231

War and Scientific Progress ............................................. 233
Significant Sub-Atomic Scientists ................................... 238
  Marie Curie (1867-1934) ............................................. 238
  Ernest Rutherford ....................................................... 238
  Niels Bohr (1885-1962) ............................................... 239
  Enrico Fermi (1901-1954) ........................................... 240
  Werner Heisenberg (1901-1976) ................................. 241
  Quantum Theorists ..................................................... 242
Biological Scientific Discoveries ....................................... 243
  Thomas H. Morgan (1866-1945) ................................. 243
  Francis Crick (1916-2004) ........................................... 243
  Francis Collins (1950- ) ............................................... 245
Modern Physics ................................................................ 245
  Albert Einstein (1879-1955) ....................................... 245
  George Lemaitre (1894-1966) .................................... 246
Quiz 9 for Chapter 9 ....................................................... 246
Chapter 10 The Cold War: Capitalism and Communism 249
  Marxism as a Response to Capitalism ......................... 253
  The Peaks of Cold War Tension .................................. 260
    Soviet Blockade in Berlin ......................................... 260
    The Korean War ....................................................... 263
    Suez Crisis and the Yom Kippur War ...................... 265
    Berlin Crisis .............................................................. 268
    Cuban Missile Crisis ................................................ 269
    Vietnam War ............................................................ 271
    War in Afghanistan .................................................. 272

The Collapse of the Soviet Union and End of the Cold
  War ..............................................................................274
  The Soviet Union's Territory..............................276
  Quiz 10 for Chapter 10 .......................................278
Chapter 11 Post-Modern Times..................................281
  Post-Modern Thought...........................................284
    Jean-François Lyotard (1924-1998)............................285
    Michel Foucault (1926-1984) and Sigmund Freud
      (1856-1939) ...........................................................287
    Jacques Derrida (1930-2004)...................................292
  Post-Modern Action..............................................294
    Student Revolts and the 1960s ................................295
    The Sexual Revolution ............................................300
  Postmodernism Architecture ..............................303
  Quiz 11 for Chapter 11 .......................................305
Chapter 12 A Multi-Centric World ............................307
  European Union.....................................................309
  Eurasian Economic Union...................................313
  India.........................................................................315
  Asian Tigers ...........................................................316
  China .......................................................................317
  Brazil.......................................................................320
  Africa ......................................................................321
  Quiz 12 for Chapter 12 .......................................325
Index ................................................................................327

# Chapter 1

## Monarchies: Limited and Checked or Supreme?

**Introduction**

From the 1600s to the 1800s, the dominant governing form of absolute rule by kings was checked, limited, and even abolished. Since the development of monarchical forms of government in France and England differ significantly, we will focus our attention on these two countries so as to provide us with the ends of the spectrum somewhere between which other European peoples' approach to monarchies fell.

Throughout a number of centuries, the English gradually and firmly moved to limiting and checking the powers of their monarch through a body known as the parliament. In contrast, France moved in the opposite direction by granting more and more power to a supreme, unchecked monarch. This accumulation of power in one individual jarringly ended in the terrible French Revolution (1789-1799) during which the French King Louis XVI and his wife Marie Antoinette were guillotined, and the monarchy was abolished. We will end this chapter with a sampling of some of the great art that was created during these turbulent, emotionally charged times.

**British Monarchy and Parliament**

The British parliament has its origins in the feudal system that William the Conqueror formed. In 1066, this Normand crossed the English Channel, from what is now northern France, to conquer the English people. On October 14th, 1066, in the Battle of Hastings, William emerged victorious and became the King of England.[1] As king, William formed a council called the *Curia Regis* with which he consulted.[2] A century and a half later, in 1215, this royal council in a Magna Carta reputedly secured authority to check the power of King John. It is debated whether this transfer of power to what would become known as the English Parliament was intended by King John.[3] As Danny Danziger argues, the belief that the Magna Carta subordinated the power of the King to the common law of England only came about centuries later when under the Stuart

---

[1] David C. Douglas, *William the Conqueror* (New Haven: Yale University Press, 1999), 6, 1055.

[2] Douglas, *William the Conqueror*, 1162.

[3] Danny Danziger, and John Gillingham, *1215: The Year of the Magna Carta* (New York: Touchstone, 2003), 270-271, 275-291.

## Chapter 1 Monarchies: Limited and Checked or Supreme?

monarchy those who wanted to increase the powers of the Parliament at the expense of the king harkened back to this document in order to bolster their claims.[4]

The English Parliament's ability to check the authority of the King was not noticeably present during the dynasty that came immediately before the Stuarts. During the Tudor reign (1485-1603), English Kings and Queens steadily consolidated power in the person of the monarch. The first Tudor to reign as King was Henry VII (reigned 1485-1509). Henry gained the crown after he successfully defeated Richard III in the War of the Roses (1455-1487).[5] King Richard III was of a rival aristocratic family called the House of York.

As King, Henry VII united the House of Tudor, which he belonged to, to the House of York by marrying a noble woman of the House of York, Elizabeth of York.[6] By uniting these two houses, Henry VII centered power in himself. When his son Henry VIII inherited the English crown he likewise further consolidated power even to the extent of rejecting papal authority and declaring himself head of the

---

[4] Danziger and Gillingham, *1215: The Year of the Magna Carta*, 270.

[5] Alison Weir, *The Wars of the Roses* (New York: Random House Publishing Group, 1995), xiii. The contestants of this war were the House of Lancaster and the House of York.

[6] Weir, *The Wars of the Roses*, 197.

Church of England in his Supremacy Act of 1534.

In 1547, Henry VIII was succeeded by his sickly son, Edward VI, who was only nine years old when he inherited the crown.[7] Six years later, Edward VI died, and, following a slightly and substantially altered legal document, the English crown passed briefly to Lady Jane Grey. It is not clear who was responsible for altering the document in order to shift the line of succession from Henry VIII's oldest daughter, Mary. Perhaps, one of Edward's councilors did so without sufficient authorization. It is very likely it occurred since Edward, who believed in Protestantism, did not want his Catholic sister Mary to inherit the crown.[8] Lady Jane Grey only reigned for a brief time, known as the "Nine Day Reign," until she was executed in 1554.[9] The next monarch of England was Henry VIII's eldest, and very Catholic, daughter Mary I (reigned 1553-1558). Upon Mary's death in 1558, her half-sister, Elizabeth, who identified herself as a Protestant, inherited the throne and ruled as Queen Elizabeth I from 1558 to 1603.

Elizabeth I's death in 1603 brought a conclusion to the tight rule of the Tudors and the beginning of the Stuart

---

[7] Jennifer Loach, *Edward VI* (Norfolk: St. Edmundsbury Press, 1999), 181.

[8] Loach, *Edward VI*, 163-164.

[9] Alison Plowden, *Lady Jane Grey* (Gloucestershire: The History Press, 2014), vi.

## Chapter 1 Monarchies: Limited and Checked or Supreme?

reign. The House of Stuart reigned over England from 1603 to 1714. As we will see, during this dynastic reign the English Parliament grew in its ability to check the power of the reigning monarch which had accumulated much power during the Tudor reign. The first Stuart to reign as King of England was James VI (reigned 1603-1625). He was succeeded by his son Charles I (reigned 1625-1649). During Charles rule, the English Parliament, or more specifically the House of Commons, demanded in its 1628 Petition of Right, in which they cited the Magna Carta, that Charles I restore their power to a supposedly more ideal time by not taxing without the consent of the Parliament, not imprisoning without just cause, not housing soldiers in homes without consent, and not issuing martial law at will.[10] Charles I agreed, but then, after a period of time of much tension with parliamentary leaders, chose to dissolve the parliament.[11] Charles I's perceived dictatorial manner of relating to the English Parliament erupted in an English Civil War between Parliamentary forces and King Charles I's military. King Charles I lost this civil war and in 1649 was execut-

---

[10] "The Petition of Right 1628," Constitution Society, http://www.constitution.org/eng/petright.htm, (accessed January 5, 2015). The Magna Carta is referred here to as the "Great Charter." For the summary of the four requests see Pauline Gregg, *King Charles I* (Berkley: University of California Press, 1981), 172

[11] Gregg, *King Charles I*, 307-310.

ed.[12]

The period that followed is often called the Interregnum (meaning 'between kings' era). It lasted from 1649 to 1660. During this short period of time, England lacked a King and instead was ruled first by Oliver Cromwell as Lord Protector (1653-1658) and then by Oliver Cromwell's son, Richard Cromwell, as Lord Protector (1658-1659).[13] The Interregnum ended in 1659 when yet another Stuart, Charles II, son of Charles I, was restored as the English King in 1660. In 1685, Charles II died but not before, interestingly, converting to the Catholic faith.[14] He was succeeded by his brother James II, who also was Catholic.

Fearing that their Catholic King would consolidate power to the detriment of Protestants, many noble Protestants resisted his rule. Their resistance came to a head when in 1688 they asked a Protestant noble from Holland, William III of Orange, to invade England and take the crown from James II. This 1688 overthrow of the Catholic King James II was named by the Protestant victors, the Glorious Revolution. A piece of legislation that Parliament insisted

---

[12] Gregg, *King Charles I*, 445.

[13] Oliver Cromwell was a distant relative of Thomas Cromwell who was the chief minister of Henry VIII until he fell out of the king's favor and was executed.

[14] Tim Harris, *Restoration: Charles II and his Kingdoms* (New York: Penguin Books, 2005), 71, 75.

that William of Orange accept before he could be named King William III was the 1689 Bill of Rights. The Bill of Rights substantially limited the powers of the English monarchs by checking the English Crown's power with Parliamentary power. See below for key sections from this document. Notice how the authors of the document associate the Catholic King, James II, with oppression of Protestants and suppression of parliamentary powers.

### ~ 1689 English Bill of Rights ~

...Whereas the late King James the Second, by the assistance of divers evil counsellors, judges and ministers employed by him, did endeavor to subvert and extirpate the Protestant religion and the laws and liberties of this kingdom;

- By assuming and exercising a power of dispensing with and suspending of laws and the execution of laws without consent of Parliament;
- ...By levying money for and to the use of the Crown by pretense of prerogative for other time and in other manner than the same was granted by Parliament;
- ...By causing several good subjects being Protestants to be disarmed at the same time

when papists were both armed and employed contrary to law;

...And thereupon the said Lords Spiritual and Temporal and Commons, pursuant to their respective letters and elections, being now assembled in a full and free representative of this nation, taking into their most serious consideration the best means for attaining the ends aforesaid, do in the first place (as their ancestors in like case have usually done) for the vindicating and asserting their ancient rights and liberties declare

- That the pretended power of suspending the laws or the execution of laws by regal authority without consent of Parliament is illegal;
- That the pretended power of dispensing with laws or the execution of laws by regal authority, as it hath been assumed and exercised of late, is illegal;
- ...That levying money for or to the use of the Crown by pretense of prerogative, without grant of Parliament, for longer time, or in other manner than the same is or shall be granted, is illegal;

- That it is the right of the subjects to petition the king, and all commitments and prosecutions for such petitioning are illegal;
- That the raising or keeping a standing army within the kingdom in time of peace, unless it be with consent of Parliament, is against law;
- That the subjects which are Protestants may have arms for their defense suitable to their conditions and as allowed by law;
- That election of members of Parliament ought to be free;
- That the freedom of speech and debates or proceedings in Parliament ought not to be impeached or questioned in any court or place out of Parliament;
- …And that for redress of all grievances, and for the amending, strengthening and preserving of the laws, Parliaments ought to be held frequently.[15]

---

[15] "English Bill of Right 1689," The Avalon Project, http://avalon.law.yale.edu/17th_century/england.asp.

## French Monarchy and Absolutism

We now will turn our attention to the country to which England had been a vassal since the time of the Norman invasion led by William the Conqueror in the eleventh century.[16] In the fourteenth century, English rulers wished to reverse this power relationship where England was subject to their French overlords. This English goal was expressed by a series of wars called the Hundred Years War (1337-1453) between England and France.[17] In one particularly famous battle, the Battle of Agincourt (1415), the English King Henry V defeated the French. Interestingly, Agincourt is only about forty miles north-west from Saint-Valery-sur Somme, the very site from which William the Conqueror embarked in order to invade and conquer England.[18]

Upon gaining victory at Agincourt, Henry V began ruling northern France. This angered the French so much that, after being inspired by St. Joan of Arc, they fought the English with great intensity.[19] Their attempt to overthrow their English rulers began in 1429 when St. Joan of Arc con-

---

[16] Douglas, *William the Conqueror*, 181-211.

[17] L. J. Andrew Villalon and Donald J. Kagay, *The Hundred Years War: A Wider Focus*, Part 1 (Boston: Brill, 2005), xxv.

[18] Douglas, *William the Conqueror*, 193, 194, 207, 396, 398.

[19] Clifford J. Rogers, "Henry V's Military Strategy in 1415," in *The Hundred Years War: A Wider Focus* eds. L.J. Andrew Villalon and Donald J. Kagay (Boston: Brill, 2005), 399-429.

## Chapter 1 Monarchies: Limited and Checked or Supreme?

vinced Charles VII, whom she recognized as the actual French King, to fight the English King, Henry VI, who only claimed to be the French King.[20] After St. Joan of Arc was captured by Burgundians, who had allied themselves with England, she was tried as a witch in an English controlled ecclesiastical court, and then, in 1431, burned at the stake.

Even though she had been executed, her vision of independence from English domination continued to inspire the French people. Finally, in the 1453 Battle of Castillon, France decisively defeated the English.[21] France's battles with England during the Hundred Years War were a principle factor that helped to cause many French people to desire a centralized state that was united and ruled by an absolute monarch who would guarantee French independence. Practically, this meant that the power of aristocrats, and other centers of power, needed to be diminished in order to centralize power in the French king. Under the French King Louis XI (reigned 1461-1483), this is precisely what occurred.[22]

The almost absolute power of the French monarch

---

[20] Villalon and Kagay, *The Hundred Years War: A Wider Focus*, Part 1, xl-xli.

[21] Villalon and Kagay, *The Hundred Years War: A Wider Focus*, Part 1, xliii.

[22] Adrianna Bakos, *Images of Kingship in Early Modern France: Louis XI in Political Thought 1560-1789* (London: Routledge, 1997), 27-60.

reached its apex in another King also named Louis, Louis XIV (reigned 1643-1715). Louis XIV's desire for power was instilled in him by his father King Louis XIII (reigned 1610 to 1643). Louis XIII continued to centralize power by eliminating rival sources of power. In order to do so, he relied heavily on his Prime Minister Cardinal Richelieu. Richelieu was devoted to transforming France into a highly, centralized state that revolved neatly around its king. Richelieu once promised King Louis XIII the following:

~ Richelieu Evaluates the State of the French Monarchy 1624 ~

> I promised your Majesty to employ all my industry and all the authority which it should please you to give me to ruin the Huguenot party [French Protestant party], to abase the pride of the nobles, to bring back all your subjects to their duty, and to elevate your name among foreign nations to the point where it belongs.[23]

Following his father's example, Louis XIV amassed so

---

[23] Richelieu, "Political Testament," in James Harvey Robinson, ed., Readings in European History (Boston: Ginn, 1904), 2:268-269.

## Chapter 1 Monarchies: Limited and Checked or Supreme?

much power that he was called the Sun King.[24] In an effort to eliminate even non-French rivals to his authority, he approved the anti-papal movement known as Gallicanism, named after the ancient Roman province of Gaul that French borders are basically based upon. According to Gallicanism, papal authority does not overrule French bishops, nor does it overrule French secular authority, above all King Louis XIV's supreme authority.[25]

Remember, at the same time Louis XIV was accumulating power, across the English Channel the English Parliament was fighting a civil war with their King Charles I. In 1649, Charles I lost the civil war and was executed. Ever since then, English Parliament has repeatedly and successfully checked the power of their monarchs. Not until 1793, in the midst of the French Revolution, did France respond in a similar way by beheading their King, Louis XVI, and his wife Queen Marie Antoinette.[26]

---

[24] See Nancy Mitford, *The Sun King* (New York: The New York Review of Books, 1967).

[25] Julius Lloyd, *The Gallican Church: Sketches of Church History in France* (London: Society for Promoting Christian Knowledge, 1879), 126.

[26] William Doyle, *The French Revolution: A Very Short Introduction* (Oxford: Oxford University Press, 2001), 52.

**Baroque Art**

We will end this chapter by looking at Baroque art that, reflecting these times, was emotionally charged. In the 1600s, Baroque art began in Italy and then spread to other European countries. The term comes from the French word *barocco* meaning a rough and imperfect pearl.[27] Originally, the term was used to indicate an unrefined artistic expression. Currently, Baroque art is not typically understood in this manner. The art created in this style, named by art historians and not by the artists themselves, often contains much hidden symbolism, freely depicts emotion, displays the human body without inhibition, is highly naturalistic, uses perspective in a very sophisticated manner, contrasts light with darkness, and focuses much attention on Roman and Greek myths. Try identifying the above characteristics in the following Baroque art.

*Gianlorenzo Bernini (1598-1680)*

Bernini was a leading Italian sculptor and architect of his times. He even considered himself, and is considered by

---

[27] William Kloss, *A History of European Art* (Chantilly: The Great Courses, 2005), 190.

others, as the successor to Michelangelo.[28] An example of his architecture is his open arm-like-embrace design of the Piazza San Pietro that is directly in front of St. Peter's Basilica. Example of his intensely emotional sculptures are the *Ecstasy of St. Teresa* of Avila and his *Apollo and Daphne* sculptor from Greek mythology.

29

---

[28] H.W. Janson, and Anthony F. Janson, *History of Art*, sixth ed. (New York: Harry N. Abrams, 2001), 541.

[29] Giovanni Battista Piranesi [Public domain], via Wikimedia Commons, "Rendition of St. Peter's Square, Rome," 1835-1839, http://commons.wikimedia.org/wiki/File%3APiranesi-16005.jpg.

---

[30] Welleschik, "The Ecstasy of St. Teresa of Avila by Bernini, located in Santa Maria della Vittoria, Rome," sculpture, 2009, http://commons.wikimedia.org/wiki/File%3ATeresa_von_Avila_Bernini1.JPG.

Chapter 1 Monarchies: Limited and Checked or Supreme?  17

*Michelangelo Merisi da Caravaggio (1571-1610)*

Caravaggio was one of Italy's foremost Baroque painters. His art is characterized by its dramatic use of light and darkness. Notice how quickly light transitions to darkness in his painting below.

---

[31] Int3gr4te, "Apollo and Daphne", painting, 2007, http://commons.wikimedia.org/wiki/File%3AApolloAndDaphne.JPG.

[32] VivaItalia1974, "Caravaggio's monumental masterpiece at the San Luigi dei Francesi church in Rome," painting, 2012,

The art historian, William Kloss points out the similarity of Michelangelo's hand of Adam in the *Creation of Adam* with the hand of Christ in the above painting by Caravaggio.[33]

*Artemisia Gentileschi (1593-1656)*

Not all of the leading Baroque Italian artists were men. Gentileschi is an example of a leading Baroque artist who was a woman. Similar to Caravaggio and Bernini she created intensely emotional art. Her painting below of Judith beheading Holofernes may have been Artemisia's way of expressing her anguish of having been once raped by a married man who had promised that he would leave his wife to marry her.[34]

---

http://commons.wikimedia.org/wiki/File%3ACaravaggio's_The_Calling_of_St_Matthew.jpg.

[33] Kloss, *A History of European Art*, 186.

[34] Keith Christiansen *Orazio and Artemisia Gentileschi* (New York: The Metropolitan Museum of Art, 2001), xv, 3.

Chapter 1 Monarchies: Limited and Checked or Supreme? 19

35

[35] Web Gallery of Art, "Judith Beheading Holofernes" painting, http://commons.wikimedia.org/wiki/File%3AArtemisia_Gentileschi_-_Judith_Beheading_Holofernes_-_WGA08565.jpg.

*Diego Velázquez (1599-1660)*

A non-Italian Baroque artist, the Spaniard, Diego Velázquez in one of his most famous paintings, *Las Meninas,* starkly contrasts light with darkness and exhibits a sophisticated ability in the use of perspective.

[36] The Yorck Project: *10.000 Meisterwerke der Malerei.* DVD-ROM, 2002. Distributed by DIRECTMEDIA Publishing GmbH, "Las Meninas (Selbstporträt mit der königlichen Familie)," painting, http://commons.wikimedia.org/wiki/File%3ADiego_Vel%C3%A1zquez_021.jpg.

Chapter 1 Monarchies: Limited and Checked or Supreme?  21

*Jean-Honoré Fragonard (1732-1806)*

The tail end of the Baroque era has been classified as the Rococo period. Rococo adds to the Baroque's emotional intensity with its playful use of curves, creamy colors, and gold. An example of this delightful, fun-filled art is *The Happy Accidents of the Swing* by the French painter Fragonard. In the painting, a pretty, young woman seated on a swing has playfully kicked her slipper off much to the delight of two men.

---

[37] http://www.wga.hu/index1.html, "The Happy Accidents of the Swing," painting, http://commons.wikimedia.org/wiki/File%3AFragonard_-_swing.jpg.

## Quiz 1 for Chapter 1

1-10. Compare and contrast how the English concept of their monarchy developed from the 1600s to the 1800s with the French concept of their monarchy during the same period. As an aid, you may use the following chart.

| English Concept of Monarchy | French Concept of Monarchy |
| --- | --- |
| 1. | 1. |
| 2. | 2. |
| 3. | 3. |
| 4. | 4. |
| 5. | 5. |

11-15. Choose one work of art from the Baroque era, which includes the Rococo, and provide the following.

    11. Name of the artist.

    12. Name of the art.

Chapter 1 Monarchies: Limited and Checked or Supreme?

13. What the artist is depicting.

14-15. Two key characteristics of the art that are seen as typical to Baroque art.

    14.

    15.

# Chapter 2

## The Rise of Western Science

**Introduction**

At the same time the dominant political form of monarchy was being re-examined, a new approach to examining the physical world was developing into a method, the scientific method.

In tracing the rise of the scientific method and explaining its concept of created matter, we will first examine how the combination of two philosophical approaches to reality, rationalism and empiricism, contributed to the foundation from which the scientific method would later develop.

Then, we will look at a number of people who promoted this method: Nicholas Copernicus, Tycho Brahe, Johannes Kepler, Galileo Galilei, Isaac Newton, and William Harvey.

We will conclude this chapter by admiring a few examples from the neoclassical artistic era that overlap with the time that the scientific rose to prominence.

## Rationalism and Empiricism

*Rene Descartes (1596-1650)*

Descartes was a French philosopher and mathematician who grounded certainty of his existence in his ability to think. In concluding this he wrote:

> ...for since I had discovered one which I knew to be true, I thought that I must likewise be able to discover the ground of this certitude. And as I observed that in the words I think, therefore I am, there is nothing at all which gives me assurance of their truth beyond this, that I see very clearly that in order to think it is necessary to exist, I concluded that I might take, as a general rule, the principle, that all the things which we very clearly and distinctly conceive are true, only observing, however, that there is some difficulty in rightly determining the objects which we distinctly conceive.[1]

---

[1] Rene Descartes, "Discourse on Method,", Project Gutenberg, http://www.gutenberg.org/files/59/59-h/59-h.htm#note, part iv, paragraph 3.

This manner of establishing truth in the individual represents a shift that was occurring during Descartes' time of relying more on the ability of the individual person to reason and less on external authority to provide reasons for individuals. The skepticism of Descartes became an element in the scientific method which does not assume that an explanation is true simply because an authority says it is, but only accepts the explanation as probable after a number of experiments yield similar results.

*Francis Bacon (1561-1626)*

Francis Bacon, a contemporary of Descartes, was an English philosopher and scientist. Bacon focused less on philosophical, logical reasoning and more on gathering empirical data in order to determine to what extent a hypothesis accurately explains reality. In his work *Novum Organum,* he attempts to find a mean between skepticism and what he refers to as a dogmatic approach to nature.[2] Both extremes can be avoided, claimed Bacon, by empirically testing in a systematic manner a proposed explanation for how a particular aspect of nature operates. Bacon explains his scientific method by writing:

---

[2] Francis Bacon, "Novum Organum," (New York: P.F. Collier and Son, MCMII), Project Gutenberg, http://www.gutenberg.org/files/45988/45988-h/45988-h.htm, preface.

We must not only search for, and procure a greater number of experiments, but also introduce a completely different method, order, and progress of continuing and promoting experience. For vague and arbitrary experience is (as we have observed), mere groping in the dark, and rather astonishes than instructs. But when experience shall proceed regularly and uninterruptedly by a determined rule, we may entertain better hopes of the sciences.[3]

**Promoters of the Scientific Method**

The empirically-based scientific method for, in the words of Francis Bacon, "determining the degrees of certainty"[4] gained many practitioners and devotees. We will now focus on a few.

*Nicholas Copernicus (1473-1543)*

The mathematician and astronomer Nicholas Copernicus was born in the Kingdom of Poland during the late fifteenth century. In his book *On the Revolutions of the Celes-*

---

[3] Francis Bacon, "Novum Organum."
[4] Francis Bacon, "Novum Organum."

# Chapter 2 The Rise of Western Science

*tial Spheres,* he supported a heliocentric theory of the universe.[5] According to the heliocentric theory of the universe, the earth and other planets revolve around the sun (in Greek *helios*) and not vice versa. This theory is an ancient one proposed as far back by a Greek mathematician and astronomer Aristarchus a few centuries before the birth of Christ.[6] According to an ancient text of the Greek mathematician and physicist Archimedes (circa 287-212 BC), Aristarchus held that:

> You are aware ['you' being King Gelon] that 'universe' is the name given by most astronomers to the sphere, the center of which is the center of the earth, while its radius is equal to the straight line between the center of the sun and the center of the earth. This is the common account ... as you have heard from the astronomers. But Aristarchus brought out a book consisting of a certain hypothesis, wherein it appears, as a consequence of the assumptions made, that the universe is many times greater than the 'uni-

---

[5] Nicholas Copernicus, *On the Revolutions of the Heavenly Spheres*, trans. Charles Glenn Wallis (Amherst: Prometheus Books, 1995).

[6] Aristarchus lived from circa 310 BC to 230 BC.

verse' just mentioned. His hypotheses are that the fixed stars and the sun remain unmoved, that the earth revolves about the sun in the circumference of a circle, the sun lying in the middle of the orbit...⁷

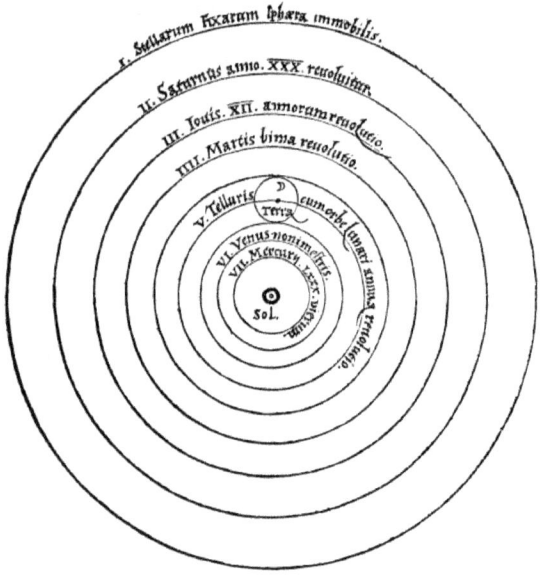

---

⁷ Thomas Heath, *Aristarchus of Samos: The Ancient Copernicus* (Oxford: Clarendon Press, 1913), 301-302. Online at https://archive.org/stream/aristarchusofsam00heatuoft#page/n5/mode/2up.

⁸ Nicolai Copernici Created in vector format by Scewing ([1]) [Public domain], via Wikimedia Commons, http://commons.wikimedia.org/wiki/File%3ACopernican_heliocentrism_theory_diagram.svg.

Chapter 2 The Rise of Western Science          31

Despite that the heliocentric theory was many, many centuries years old, most scientists at the time of Copernicus held that the sun revolves around the earth. This geocentric model was very early on proposed by Ptolemy (circa 90-168 AD), a Greco-Egyptian. Above is a seventeenth-century painting of the Ptolemaic earth-centered model. Compare this explanation of the universe with the Copernican, sun (*sol*)-centered model below.

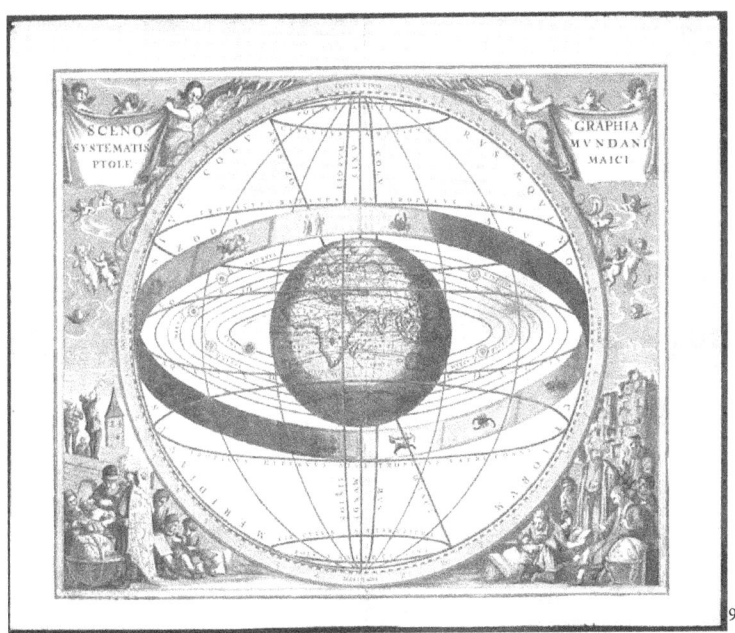

Unlike in the case of Galileo Galilei, the Catholic

---

[9] By Loon, J. van (Johannes), ca. 1611–1686. (http://nla.gov.au/nla.map-nk10241) [Public domain], via Wikimedia Commons, http://commons.wikimedia.org/wiki/File%3ACellarius_ptolemaic_system.jpg.

Church did not correct Copernicus. This was because, Copernicus did not present his heliocentric view as a fact but rather as a possible explanation that was not sufficiently proven. The Church's acceptance of Copernicus' research is apparent in the foreword to his 1543 book *On the Revolutions of the Celestial Spheres*. The foreword contains a 1536 letter from Cardinal Schönberg, which reads:

~ Cardinal Schönberg 1536 letter to Copernicus ~

> Some years ago word reached me concerning your proficiency, of which everybody constantly spoke. At that time I began to have a very high regard for you, and also to congratulate our contemporaries among whom you enjoyed such great prestige. For I had learned that you had not merely mastered the discoveries of the ancient astronomers uncommonly well but had also formulated a new cosmology. In it you maintain that the earth moves; that the sun occupies the lowest, and thus the central, place in the universe; that the eighth heaven remain perpetually motionless and fixed; and that, together with the elements included in its sphere, the moon, situated between the heavens of Mars and Venus, revolves around

## Chapter 2 The Rise of Western Science

the sun in the period of a year. I have also learned that you have written an exposition of this whole system of astronomy, and have computed the planetary motions and set them down in tables, to the greatest admiration of all. Therefore with the utmost earnestness I entreat you, most learned sir, unless I inconvenience you, to communicate this discovery of yours to scholars, and at the earliest possible moment to send me your writings on the sphere of the universe together with the tables and whatever else you have that is relevant to this subject. Moreover, I have instructed Theodoric of Reden to have everything copied in your quarters at my expense and dispatched to me. If you gratify my desire in this matter, you will see that you are dealing with a man who is zealous for your reputation and eager to do justice to so fine a talent. Farewell.[10]

---

[10] Nicholas Copernicus, *On the Revolutions*, trans. Edward Rosen (Baltimore: John Hopkins University Press, 2008), WebExibits, http://www.webexhibits.org/calendars/year-text-Copernicus.html; In 1616, after Copernicus had died, the Catholic Church decided for prudential reasons to place Copernicus's book *On the Revolutions of the Celestial Spheres* on the Index. In 1835, this book was finally removed from the Index. Jack Rep-

*Tycho Brahe (1546-1601)*

Tycho Brahe was a Danish astronomer who disagreed with both the Ptolemaic, geocentric model and the Copernican, heliocentric model. His model for explaining the universe is a combination of these two models. His model has since been disproven. See below for his hybrid, Tychonic model.

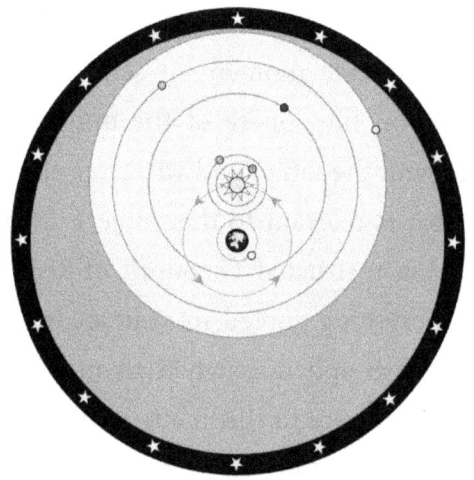

check, *Copernicus' Secret: How the Scientific Revolution Began* (New York: Simon & Schuster, 2007), 194.

[11] User:Fastfission, "Diagram depicting the basics of the Tychonian geocentric system. Basically, the objects on blue orbits (the Moon and the Sun and the fixed stars) revolve around the Earth. The objects on orange orbits (Mercury, Venus, Mars, Jupiter, and Saturn) revolve around the Sun. All is surrounded by a sphere of fixed stars (though they are fixed only with respect to each other, for the sphere revolves around the earth). The system

## Johannes Kepler (1571-1630) and Galileo Galilei (1564-1642)

The German astronomer Johannes Kepler, although respectful of Tycho Brahe's observations, built his "whole astronomy upon Copernicus's hypothesis concerning the world."[12] He improved Copernicus's heliocentric model by incorporating elliptical orbits into the explanation thereby more accurately identifying and predicting planetary orbits.

---

is essentially geocentric, though everything except for the moon and the fixed stars and the earth centre itself revolves around the Sun. Distances are of course just generalized, though it is important that the minor planets are always "tied" to the Sun while the major planets can be on either side of the Earth. This is a superior diagram of Tycho's system to most that you will find: the path of the sun's orbit intersects with the path of Mars' orbit, causing a problem for any astronomer thinking of the mechanism as incorporating nested physical "spheres"," diagram, http://commons.wikimedia.org/wiki/File%3ATychonian_system.svg.

[12] Johannes Kepler, *Epitome of Copernican Astronomy and Harmonies of the World*, trans. Charles Glenn Wallis (Amherst: Prometheus Books, 1995), 10.

*Kepler's Laws*

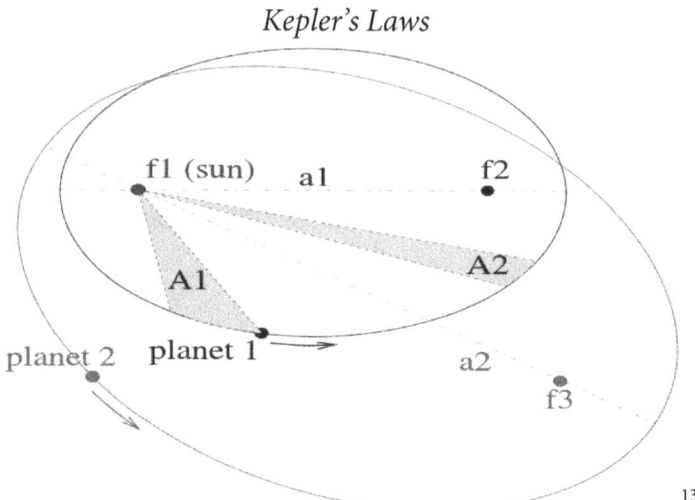

The Italian astronomer Galileo Galilei also backed Copernicus' explanation for how the planets and stars interact with one another. Unfortunately, in promoting Copernicus's hypothesis, Galileo took liberties to mock those, including the Pope, who wanted Galileo to be more cautious in how he presented this hypothesis. Many held that there

---

[13] Hankwang, "Diagram illustrating Kepler's laws. Figure 1: Illustration of Kepler's three laws with two planetary orbits. (1) The orbits are ellipses, with focal points $f1$ and $f2$ for the first planet and $f1$ and $f3$ for the second planet. The Sun is placed in focal point $f1$. (2) The two shaded sectors $A1$ and $A2$ have the same surface area and the time for planet 1 to cover segment $A1$ is equal to the time to cover segment $A2$. (3) The total orbit times for planet 1 and planet 2 have a ratio $a13/2 : a23/2$.," diagram, https://commons.wikimedia.org/wiki/File%3AKepler_laws_diagram.svg.

was not sufficient evidence for Copernicus's hypothesis. Furthermore, since Galileo lived during the time when Protestant Reformers were teaching *Sola Scriptura,* the Catholic Church did not want to even appear to promote as an established fact a hypothesis that contradicted scripture's phenomenological description of the sun rotating around the earth. Not heeding or respecting Church officials' caution, Galileo wrote a book, *Dialogue Concerning the Two Chief World Systems,* in which the character *Simplicio* (simpleton) speaks words that the reigning Pope, Urban VIII, had actually said.[14] Galileo's mockery of the papacy angered Pope Urban VIII so much that within a relatively short time Galileo was brought to trial, found suspect of heresy, forced to recant and placed under house arrest.[15]

*Isaac Newton (1642-1727)*

The English mathematician and physicist Isaac Newton, born on the same year that Galileo died, relied on both Galileo's research and theories and Kepler's research and

---

[14] Galileo Galilei, *Dialogue Concerning the Two Chief World Systems*, trans. Stillman Drake (New York: The Modern Library, 2001), xvi.

[15] Galileo Galilei, *Dialogue Concerning the Two Chief World Systems*, xiii-xxiii.

theories in order to develop his own.¹⁶ Studying Kepler's laws of planetary motion greatly helped Newton to formulate laws on motion and on gravitation.¹⁷ Newton's three laws of motion are all based on one principle: material things move according to the same physical laws. This foundational principle that seems obvious to our modern ears was not obvious at the time of Newton. During Newton's age, many scientists followed Aristotle's assumptions that bodies that are heavy tend to go downwards, bodies that are light tend to go upwards, the stars and planets move in circles, and that in order for something to be moved motion needs to be continually imparted to it.¹⁸ Aristotle's conclusions are based on what he observed with his senses. For example, what motion do you expect from smoke and what motion do you expect from a rock that is

---

[16] Richard S. Westfall, *The Life of Isaac Newton* (Cambridge: Cambridge University Press, 1993), 1, 50, 138, 152, 159, 164, and 167.

[17] A. Rupert Hall, *Isaac Newton: Adventurer in Thought* (Cambridge: Cambridge University Press, 1992), 38, 76; Peter Guthrie Tait, *Treatise on Natural Philosophy*, Vol. 1 (Oxford: Clarendon Press, 1867), 179-184.

[18] Aristotle, *Physics*, trans. Robin Waterfield (Oxford: Oxford University Press, 2008), 35, 43, 57, 88-90; "The Physics of Aristotle versus the Physics of Galileo," Dept. Physics & Astronomy University of Tennessee, http://csep10.phys.utk.edu/astr161/lect/history/aristotle_dynamics.html.

dropped? Challenging Aristotle's "call it as you see it" approach to nature, Newton argued that every material object continues in either a state of rest or motion unless affected by force: the degree of change in motion of an object in motion is proportional to the force acting on it, and every action always entails an equal and opposite reaction.[19]

*William Harvey (1578-1657)*

We now turn our attention to a scientist, the English physicist William Harvey, who did not focus his intelligence in explaining how the stars and planets move but rather how the human body functions, specifically how blood circulates from the heart to the body and back to the heart. See below for two drawings in his book *On the Motion of the Heart and Blood*. The illustrations depict the veins of the human arm to demonstrate that the vein's valves only allow blood to flow in one direction. Harvey's discoveries challenged another view of the time that can be traced back to Galen. According to the ancient Greek physician Galen (circa 129-216 AD), the liver produces blood.[20]

---

[19] Isaac Newton, *The Mathematical Principles of Natural Philosophy*, trans. Andrew Motte (London: Middle-Temple-Gate, MDCCXXIX), 19-21.

[20] http://wellcomeimages.org/indexplus/obf_images/b1/54/d9f548efa6525d3ad491740cccbf.jpg, "'De Motu Cordis', by Wil-

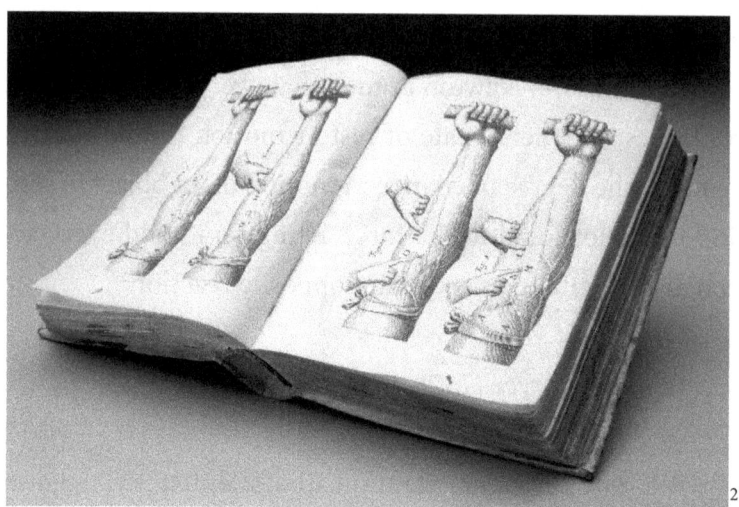

liam Harvey, Frankfurt, Germany, 162. William Harvey (1578-1657), an English physician, was the first person to accurately describe the circulation of blood pumped by the heart. This was one of the most important anatomical discoveries of the Renaissance. These famous illustrations – the only ones in the book – show experiments made on the veins to prove the presence of valves that permit blood flow in one direction only. Most traditional views about blood and its circulation, prior to this time, originated with Galen, who had believed that blood was produced in the liver." Drawing, http://commons.wikimedia.org/wiki/File%3A'De_Motu_Cordis'_%2C_by_William_Harvey%2C_Frankfurt%2C_Germany%2C_162_Wellcome_L0060483.jpg.

[21] Ibid. http://wellcomeimages.org/indexplus/obf_images/b1/54/d9f548efa6525d3ad491740cccbf.jpg, "'De Motu Cordis', by William Harvey, Frankfurt, Germany, 162.

## Neo-Classical Art

The art that coincides with the rise of the scientific method is called neo-classical because, once again, artists were inspired by ancient Greek and Roman art. Below are a few examples of neo-classical artists and their art.

*Jacques-Louis David (1748-1825)*

Jacques-Louis David was a French painter who adopted the Neoclassical Style and not the highly decorative Rococo style to which you were introduced earlier. The first painting, *The Oath of Horatii* (1785), is based on an ancient Roman legend recorded in Livy's *History of Rome*. According to this legend, the people of Rome and the people of Alba decided to settle a feud by choosing three men from each city. Once chosen, the three men from the city of Rome were to fight the three men from the city of Alba. The painting below depicts three brothers from the city of Rome of the house of Horatii who have been chosen to fight on behalf of their city. They are seen saluting their father.[22]

---

[22] William Kloss, *A History of European Art* (Chantilly: The Great Courses, 2005), 249.

23

The next painting by David, *Death of Socrates* (1787), also depicts a snapshot from ancient life but this time from Greece. The great philosopher Socrates was found guilty of corrupting Athenian young with bad ideas. His punishment was to kill himself by drinking hemlock.[24]

---

[23] wartburg.edu, "The Oath of the Horatii," painting, http://commons.wikimedia.org/wiki/File%3AJacques-Louis_David%2C_Le_Serment_des_Horaces.jpg.

[24] H.W. Janson, and Anthony F. Janson, *History of Art*, sixth ed. (New York: Harry N. Abrams, 2001), 642.

Chapter 2 The Rise of Western Science                43

25

*Antonio Canova (1757-1822)*

Antonio Canova was an Italian sculptor of the Neo-Classical style. Below is an example of one of his works, *Cupid Kisses Psyche*. This painting was inspired by a myth that appears in the Latin novel *Metamorphoses* by Apuleius (124-170 AD).[26]

---

[25] http://www.metmuseum.org/collection/the-collection-online/search/436105, "The Death of Socrates by Jacques-Louis David," painting, http://commons.wikimedia.org/wiki/File%3A David_-_The_Death_of_Socrates.jpg.

[26] Lucius Apuleius, "The Golden Asse," trans. William Adlington, chap. 22, Gutenberg, http://www.gutenberg.org/files/1666/1666-h/1666-h.htm#link2H_4_0029.

44　Western Civilization: Renaissance to Modern Times

27

*Benjamin Latrobe (1764-1820)*

Benjamin Latrobe was a British neoclassical architect who immigrated to the USA. In the US, he fostered an American neoclassical style. Below is one of his most famous works, the Baltimore Basilica of the National Shrine

---

[27] Jörg Bittner Unna, "Amor (Cupid) kisses Psyche by Antonio Canova," painting, http://commons.wikimedia.org/wiki/File%3AAmor-Psyche-Canova-JBU01.JPG.

of the Assumption of the Blessed Virgin Mary.[28]

---

[28] H.W. Janson, and Anthony F. Janson, *History of Art*, sixth ed. (New York: Harry N. Abrams, 2001), 697-698.

[29] Basilica1, "The Baltimore Basilica of the National Shrine of the Assumption of the Blessed Virgin Mary, by night, designed by Benjamin Latrobe," architecture, http://commons.wikimedia.org/wiki/File%3AExt-Night.jpg.

## Quiz 2 for Chapter 2

1-3. Explain in three ways how both rationalism and empiricism helped in the development of the scientific method.

    1.

    2.

    3.

4-7. Choose one of the following scientists: Nicholas Copernicus, Tycho Brahe, Johannes Kepler, Galileo Galilei, Isaac Newton, and William Harvey. In a minimum of four sentences, explain how this scientist contributed to scientific inquiry.

8-9. Why was Galileo corrected by the Catholic Church while Copernicus was not? After all, they both held that the earth revolves around the sun. Provide two reasons.

# Chapter 2 The Rise of Western Science

8.


9.


10-14. Choose one work of art from the Neo-Classical era and do the following.

    10. Name of the artist.


    11. Name of the art.



    12. What the artist is depicting.



13-14. Name two key characteristics of the art that are typically seen in Neo-Classical art.

    13.


    14.

# Chapter 3

## Politics and Revolutions

**Introduction**

The heightened scientific development in the Western World covered in the previous chapter has been called a revolution. In this chapter, we will be studying actual revolutions that were not simply confined to how the human mind perceives reality. First, we will discuss the American Revolution; then, we will examine the French Revolution. Interspersed in our examination of these two political revolutions will be references to key philosophers of these times whose ideas helped to influence Western political reality, namely Thomas Hobbes, John Locke, Montesquieu, and Jean-Jacques Rousseau. We will conclude this chapter with Romantic art that roughly was an expression of revolutionary sentiment.

**American Revolution**

In September of 1774, fifty five delegates from twelve British colonies (the colony of Georgia was absent) met at Philadelphia for the First Continental Congress to decide how to respond to the British Parliament's passing of the Coercive Acts.[1] The British Parliament passed the 1774 Coercive Acts as a way to punish the colonist's rebellious actions, especially for the incident known as the Boston Tea Party. Included in the acts was the closing of the Boston port until tea destroyed by American colonists was compensated for.[2]

During the Boston Tea Party incident of December 16, 1773, colonists protested the British Tea Act of 1773, which allowed the British East India Company to sell its tea duty free to the colonies while taxing the tea when it landed in colonial ports. Dressed up as Native Americans, colonists boarded British ships docked in Boston and proceeded to throw the British tea in the ocean.[3] In throwing the tea into Boston Harbor, the colonists were not only expressing their anger against the Tea Act but also against a similar act passed by the British Parliament in 1765, the Stamp Act. According to the Stamp Act, if colonists wished to print on paper, they were required to first purchase officially stamped paper manufactured in England.[4]

---

[1] Gordon S. Wood, *The American Revolution a History* (New York: Random House, 2002), 48.

[2] Wood, *The American Revolution a History*, viii, 38.

[3] Wood, *The American Revolution a History*, 37.

[4] Number one of the Stamp Act reads, "For every skin or piece of vellum or parchment, or sheet or piece of paper, on which shall be engrossed, written, or printed, any declaration,

## Chapter 3 Politics and Revolution

By 1775, thirteen colonies had mutually rejected the authority of the British Parliament on the grounds that the American colonies were being governed without representation. They then began governing themselves with provincial congresses and a Continental Congress.[5] Not surprisingly, the British responded to the colonies by sending troops. In 1775, the American Revolutionary War had begun.[6] Soon afterwards, on July 4th, 1776, the American Declaration of Independence, drafted by Thomas Jefferson, was officially promulgated by the Continental Congress. The Declaration of Independence explicitly refers to God and a moral law that is reflective of His nature. See below.

> When in the Course of human events, it becomes necessary for one people to dissolve the political bands which have connected them with another, and to assume among the powers of the earth, the separate and equal station to which the Laws of Nature and of Nature's God entitle them, a decent

---

plea, replication, rejoinder, demurrer or other pleading, or any copy thereof; in any court of law within the British colonies and plantations in America, a stamp duty of *three pence*." "The Stamp Act," US History, http://www.ushistory.org/declaration/related/stampact.htm.

[5] Wood, *The American Revolution a History*, 48.

[6] Wood, *The American Revolution a History*, 53.

respect to the opinions of mankind requires that they should declare the causes which impel them to the separation.[7]

George Washington, as Commander, led the American side to victory. Very likely, American victory would have been impossible without the help of the French. In 1778, the French, who had been longtime rivals of Britain, agreed to help the Americans both on land and on sea.[8] The decisive 1781 defeat of the British at Yorktown, Virginia, was completed by a coalition of American and French forces.[9] On September 3rd, 1783, the British admitted defeat at the hands of their former colonies.[10]

Within a decade, a number of foundational US documents were written and approved, in particular the 1788 US Constitution that replaced the former Articles of Confederation and Perpetual Union, and the 1791 US Bill of Rights, which consists of the first ten amendments to the US Constitution.[11] Since then, 17 more amendments to the US Constitution have been added. Now that we have covered

---

[7] "Declaration of Independence," The Charters of Freedom, http://www.archives.gov/exhibits/charters/declaration_transcript.html.

[8] Wood, *The American Revolution a History*, xv

[9] Wood, *The American Revolution a History*, xvi.

[10] Wood, *The American Revolution a History*, xvi.

[11] Wood, *The American Revolution a History*, xvii.

Chapter 3 Politics and Revolution

the essential events of the American Revolution, we will turn to two key philosophers who influenced the early formation of American thought on government: John Locke and Charles-Louis de Secondat, Baron de La Brède et de Montesquieu, or, more familiarly, just Montesquieu.

*John Locke (1632-1704)*

John Locke was such an influential philosopher for the leaders of the American colonists who rose up in revolt against the British that he has been named as "the philosopher of the American Revolution." Locke's *Two Treatises of Government* was a particularly influential work. Another influential work was his *An Essay Concerning Human Understanding*. Compare two passages from these work on the left with words from the 1776 US Declaration of Independence.

| John Locke | US Declaration of Independence |
|---|---|
| Man being born, as has been proved with a title to perfect freedom, and an uncontrolled enjoyment of all the rights and privileges of Law of Nature, equally with any other man or | **We hold these truths to be self-evident, that all men are created equal, that they are endowed by their Creator with certain unalienable Rights that** |

| | |
|---|---|
| number of man in the world, hath by nature a power, not only to preserve his property, that is, his **life, liberty and estate** against the injuries and attempts of other men; but to judge of and punish the breaches of that Law in others, as he is persuaded the offence deserves, even with death itself, in crimes where the heinousness of the fact, in his opinion requires it.[12] | among these are Life, Liberty and the pursuit of Happiness.[13] |

---

[12] John Locke, *Two Treatises on Government*, student edition (Cambridge: Cambridge University Press, 1988), no. 87, 323-324.

[13] "Declaration of Independence," The Charters of Freedom, http://www.archives.gov/exhibits/charters/declaration_transcript.html. In Locke's social contract theory, which greatly influenced the U.S. founders, the state offers security to its citizens in exchange for the citizens' submission to the state which tends to be run by the wealthiest. Happiness, consequently, tends to be defined by how much wealth an individual has after successfully pursuing and accumulating it. "The pursuit of happiness" can be reasonably interpreted as promoting the belief that happiness is defined by pursuing wealth. In contrast, the early and medieval

## Chapter 3 Politics and Revolution

*Below is an excerpt from John Locke's An Essay Concerning Human Understanding, The Necessity of pursuing true Happiness the Foundation of Liberty.*

> As therefore the highest perfection of intellectual nature lies in a careful and constant pursuit of true and solid happiness; so the care of ourselves, that we mistake not imaginary for real happiness, is the necessary foundation of our liberty. The stronger ties we have to an unalterable pursuit of happiness in general, which is our greatest good, and which as such, our desires always follow, the more are we free from any necessary determination of our will to any particular action, and from a necessary compliance with

---

Church view was that happiness is the vision of God in the next life that we can anticipate here as we are making a pilgrimage to our heavenly homeland. Chad Pecknold, *Christianity and Politics* (Eugene: Wipf and Stock, 2010), 120. Here Pecknold states, "It is no surprise then that in the Lockean views of Thomas Jefferson, a largely mercantilist vision translated the 'pursuit of happiness' as the pursuit of private economic interests. Happiness had once been associated, in the early and medieval church, with the vision of God. Now happiness had been reduced to a pursuit rather than a pilgrimage. Life, liberty and the pursuit of happiness would be found through hard work and economic production."

our desire, so upon any particular, and then appearing preferable good, till we have duly examined whether it has a tendency to, or be inconsistent with, our real happiness: and therefore, till we are as much informed upon this inquiry as the weight of the matter, and the nature of the case demands, we are, by the necessity of preferring and pursuing true happiness as our greatest good, obliged to suspend the satisfaction of our desires in particular cases.[14]

*Montesquieu (1689-1755)*

The French attorney and philosopher Montesquieu theorized on a political system made up of three relatively distinct powers that check and balance one another. The three powers Montesquieu separated from one another in order for each one to check the other two are as follows: executive, legislative, and judicial.[15] The American political

---

[14] John Locke, *An Essay Concerning Human Understanding*, volume I (George in Fleet Street: Eliz. Holt, for Thomas Basset, 1689), No. 52. Project Gutenberg, http://www.gutenberg.org/cache/epub/10615/pg10615.html.

[15] Montesquieu, *The Spirit of the Laws*, trans. Anne M. Cohler (Cambridge: Cambridge University Press, 1989), xxv, 132, 156, 162, 164, 169, 182.

system reflects his thought by granting executive power to the President, judicial power to the courts, and legislative power to the two houses of congress, the Senate and the House of Representatives.

**Philosophy of the French Revolution**

As Locke's ideas served as the philosophy of the American Revolution and the Founding Fathers of the U.S., Jean-Jacques Rousseau's ideas served as the philosophy of the French Revolution. The historian Jonathan Steinberg in reference to the founding days of the U.S. asserts that Rousseau's idea of a Social Contract to which he refers in *The Social Contract*, with the General Will as its basis, "was precisely what the founding Fathers [of the U.S.A] rejected, and the Constitution of 1787 was designed to prevent [such a] democracy, not encourage it."[16] According to the German philosopher Hannah Arendt, Rousseau's idea of a General Will was specifically adopted by French revolutionaries, who, in order establish a single political will, violently killed those who did not agree with their mandated

---

[16] Jonathan Steinberg, *European History and European Lives: 1715 to 1914*, CDs and Course Guidebook (Chantilly: Great Courses, 2003), 37.

political will.[17] Compare the two passages below on the idea of a General Will first written by Rousseau in 1762 and then adopted by the Revolutionary writers of France's 1789 *Declaration of the Rights of Man and the Citizen*. What do you think Rousseau meant by forcing citizens to be free? As explained by Lawrence Cahoone, Rousseau is basing this concept on his division between a lower self and a "higher, true self."[18] The higher true self is determined by the General Will. People will only be truly free if they follow their higher self, determined by the General Will similarly as drug addicts experience true freedom when they follow their higher self that does not want to choose drugs.[19] How do you think the French Revolutionaries interpreted this concept of Rousseau?

~ *Rousseau's General Will* ~

As soon as this multitude is so united in one body, it is impossible to offend against one

---

[17] Hannah Arendt, *On Revolution*, trans. (New York: Penguin Books Ltd., 2006), 66-69.

[18] Lawrence Cahoon, *The Modern Political Tradition: Hobbes to Habermas, Lectures 1-18* (Chantilly: The Teaching Company, 2014), 110.

[19] Cahoon, *The Modern Political Tradition: Hobbes to Habermas, Lectures 1-18*, 110.

of the members without attacking the body, and still more to offend against the body without the members resenting it. Duty and interest therefore equally oblige the two contracting parties to give each other help; and the same men should seek to combine, in their double capacity, all the advantages dependent upon that capacity.

... In order then that the social compact may not be an empty formula, it tacitly includes the undertaking, which alone can give force to the rest, that whoever refuses to obey the general will shall be compelled to do so by the whole body. This means nothing less than that he will be forced to be free; for this is the condition which, by giving each citizen to his country, secures him against all personal dependence. In this lies the key to the working of the political machine; this alone legitimizes civil undertakings, which, without it, would be absurd, tyrannical, and liable to the most frightful abuses.[20]

---

[20] Jean-Jacques Rousseau, "The Social Contract" (1762), Book 1, Section 7, Project Gutenberg, http://www.gutenberg.org/files/46333/46333-h/46333-h.htm.

## ~ Article Six of the Declaration of the Rights of Man ~

Law is the expression of the general will.[21] Every citizen has a right to participate personally, or through his representative, in its foundation. It must be the same for all, whether it protects or punishes. All citizens, being equal in the eyes of the law, are equally eligible to all dignities and to all public positions and occupations, according to their abilities, and without distinction except that of their virtues and talents.[22]

---

[21] Contrast this definition of law with, "Law is a rule of conduct enacted by competent authority for the sake of the common good. The moral law presupposes the rational order, established among creatures for their good and to serve their final end, by the power, wisdom, and goodness of the Creator. All law finds its first and ultimate truth in the eternal law. Law is declared and established by reason as a participation in the providence of the living God, Creator and Redeemer of all. "Such an ordinance of reason is what one calls law." 1951 [cf. St. Thomas Aquinas, STH I-II, 90,1.] "Catechism of the Catholic Church, paragraph 1951," http://www.vatican.va/archive/ccc_css/archive/catechism/p3s1c3a1.htm.

[22] Article Six of the *Declaration of the Rights of Man*. Declaration of the Rights of Man – 1789, The Avalon Project, Yale Law School, http://avalon.law.yale.edu/18th_century/rightsof.asp.

## The Four Governments of the French Revolution

During the French revolution, France was governed by four distinct ruling bodies: The National Constituent Assembly (1789-1791), The Legislative Assembly (1791-1792), The National Convention (1792-1795), and The Directory (1795-1799).[23]

### 1. The National Constituent Assembly (1789-1791)

Prior to The National Constituent Assembly, France was ruled by the absolute monarch, King Louis XVI (1754-1793), who was referred to, along with his wife Marie Antoinette, in a previous chapter. In order to disadvantage England, whom the French viewed as a competitor, King Louis XVI agreed to financially back the Americans during the American Revolutionary war (1775-1783), but only when he was convinced he was backing the winning side. Interestingly, by so doing he prepared the way for his own power to be undermined. This was because the heroic fight of the American colonists to rid themselves of being ruled by the British King George III inspired French people to

---

[23] For the explanation of the French Revolution, I basically follow the explanation, with some modification, that I provided in my book *Catholic Church History* (St. Louis: En Route Books & Media, 2018) from the time of the Protestant Reformation.

overthrow their own king.[24]

In addition, in order to help the Americans King Louis XVI put his country into further debt, thus giving more reasons for his people to dislike him and to revolt against him.[25] After the Americans, in part relying on French financial resources, had successfully defeated the British, King Louis XVI set about finding ways to pay off French debt that had become exacerbated by a season of poor crops and inflated food prices. In 1789, he called together a political body, inactive since 1614, called the Estates-General.[26] The Estates-General consisted of three estates: First Estate (clergy), Second Estate (nobles), and Third Estate (made up of lawyers, businessmen, and peasants).

On June 15th of 1789, the members, including clergy, voted to change the name from The Estates-General to the National Assembly. The name change was done in order to indicate that the National Assembly was autonomous from the King. Not surprisingly, the King and his counsel responded five days later on June 20th, 1789, by locking out the assembly members from the building in which they were holding their meetings. In great anger, the assembly members, joined by "a majority of the clergy representa-

---

[24] Linda S. Frey and Marsha L. Frey, *The French Revolution* (Westport: Greenwood Press, 2004), 24.

[25] Frey and Frey, *The French Revolution*, 24.

[26] Frey and Frey, *The French Revolution*, 3.

tives" and three nobles, held their scheduled meeting in a nearby tennis court.[27] At the tennis court, the assembly solemnly swore a "Tennis Court Oath" in which they reaffirmed that France's ruling body was the National Assembly of France and not the King and his counsel.[28]

Soon after the Tennis Court Oath was taken, King Louis XVI fired his finance minister Jacques Necker. The firing of Necker further incited French people against the King since Necker, who had advocated increasing the Third Estate's representation, was believed to be on the side of the poor.[29] In response to Necker's firing, out of frustration for the high cost of food, and in irritation over the stalemate in government, Parisians began rioting and looting. Their mayhem peaked when a mob attacked the Bastille state prison on July 14th, 1789. There the mob set free the Bastille's seven prisoners: a nobleman, two severely mentally ill people, and four forgers.[30] In an irrational frenzy, the mob murdered the governor of the Bastille, murdered the city's chief magistrate, chopped off both of their heads, and proceeded to parade around with the heads of the governor

---

[27] William Doyle, *Oxford History of the French Revolution*, Second Edition (Oxford: Oxford University, 2002), 105-106.

[28] Doyle, *Oxford History of the French Revolution*, Second Edition, 105-106.

[29] Frey and Frey, *The French Revolution*, 3.

[30] Simon Schama, *Citizens: A Chronicle of the French Revolution* (New York: Vintage Books, 1989), 392.

and magistrate stuck on pikes.[31]

Cooler minded revolutionaries set about to fundamentally change the laws of France. In August of 1789, the National Constituent Assembly issued The Declaration of the Rights of Man, which we covered previously. During the following year of 1790, the National Constituent Assembly turned against another group of people, the Catholic clergy, whom they classified as favoring the King and his aristocrats. In order to repress Catholicism in France, the Assembly prohibited the profession of monastic vows and issued a civil constitution of the clergy. According to this constitution, clergy were to be paid by public funds, priests and bishops were to be elected by the people, and all clerics were to swear an oath of obedience to the constitution.[32] Other anti-Church legislation passed during the reign of the Assembly included ending in 1789 the tithe (tax) that was given to the Church, and the 1789 authorization to sell off Catholic Church land in order to grow the coffers of the revolutionary French Government.[33]

---

[31] Doyle, *Oxford History of the French Revolution*, Second Edition, 112.

[32] William Doyle, *The French Revolution: A Very Short Introduction* (Oxford: Oxford University Press, 2001), 46-47.

[33] Nigel Aston, *Religion and Revolution in France, 1780-1804* (London: MacMillan Press, 2000), 127, 133.

## 2. The Legislative Assembly (1791-1792)

In 1791, the Legislative Assembly that replaced the National Constituent Assembly set about persecuting the Catholic Church with even greater intensity. Religious orders that either taught or worked in hospitals were suppressed.[34] The state replaced the Church's civic responsibility of keeping registers of births, marriages, and deaths.[35] Clerical attire was forbidden. Church funds and property were seized by the government,[36] and priests who refused to take an oath of fidelity to the constitution were, if captured, imprisoned or killed.[37] The excerpt below, from the 1791 Constitution, demonstrates the Assembly's dislike and restriction of both ecclesial power and inherited power.

~ Selections from the French Constitution of 1791 ~

> The National Assembly, wishing to establish the French Constitution upon the principles it has just recognized and declared, abolishes irrevocably the institutions which were injurious to liberty and equality of rights.

---

[34] Aston, *Religion and Revolution in France, 1780-1804*, 182.

[35] Aston, *Religion and Revolution in France, 1780-1804*, 183.

[36] Aston, *Religion and Revolution in France, 1780-1804*, 182.

[37] Aston, *Religion and Revolution in France, 1780-1804*, 182.

Neither nobility, nor peerage, nor hereditary distinctions, nor distinctions of orders, nor feudal regime, nor patrimonial courts, nor any titles, denominations, or prerogatives derived therefrom, nor any order of knighthood, nor any corporations or decorations requiring proofs of nobility or implying distinctions of birth, nor any superiority other than that of public functionaries in the performance of their duties any longer exists.

....

The law no longer recognizes religious vows or any other obligation contrary to natural rights or the Constitution.

...

Chapter II

....

3. There is no authority in France superior to that of the law; the King reigns only thereby, and only in the name of the law may he exact obedience.[38]

---

[38] "French Constitution of 1791," World History Project, http://worldhistoryproject.org/1791/9/3/french-constitution-of-1791.

Within about a year's time this second governing body began fracturing apart. The reason was that the three political parties that made up the Legislative Assembly began fighting one another.[39] One party (the *Feuillants*)[40] supported inherited, royal power, another party (the *Girondins* also known as the *Brissotins* or the *Rolandins*)[41] wanted royal power to be gradually checked, and the third party (the *Jacobins*) wanted to suddenly change the government by eliminating the last remaining features of inherited, royal power.[42] The latter party, the *Jacobins* and most radical of the three parties, overpowered the other two to form yet another governing body, the National Convention.

### 3. The National Convention (1792-1795)

After gaining control of the French Government, the Jacobins issued inclusive voting laws for how representatives to the National Convention were to be chosen. Previously, during the reign of the Legislative Assembly, only wealthy landowners were allowed to be electors. Once these electors were chosen by a general population vote, they

---

[39] Frey and Frey, *The French Revolution*, 165.
[40] Frey and Frey, *The French Revolution*, 165.
[41] Frey and Frey, *The French Revolution*, 163-164.
[42] Frey and Frey, *The French Revolution*, 6.

then voted who would be the nation's representatives.[43] The National Convention also greatly reduced the power of the wealthy and aristocratic by abolishing King Louis XVI's rule, which had been suspended. Once King Louis XVI was removed from office, the National Convention charged him with high treason, and placed him on trial. The King's failed attempt to flee France in June of 1791 convinced the court of his guilt by a verdict that passed by only one vote.[44] On January 21, 1793 the King was guillotined.[45]

Upon hearing of the French King's execution, England, the Dutch Republic, Italian States, and Spain joined the Holy Roman Emperor in a war against France.[46] A few months later, on October 16th, 1793, Queen Marie Antoinette was also guillotined, but not before she underwent a brutal, character assassination campaign. She was accused of being a lesbian,[47] and of being completely uncaring for the poor of France. Even today, a phrase indicating her coldness is still unjustly attributed to her, "Let them eat cake." There is no documentary proof that the Queen ever said these

---

[43] "French Constitution of 1791," World History Project, http://worldhistoryproject.org/1791/9/3/french-constitution-of-1791.

[44] Doyle, *The French Revolution*, 47.

[45] Doyle, *The French Revolution*, 52.

[46] Doyle, *The French Revolution*, 52.

[47] Vincent Cronin, *Louis and Antoinette* (London: Harvill Press, 1996), 402, 404.

words.[48]

The same year that the Queen was executed, a horrific time began, the Reign of Terror (1793-1794) spearheaded by the attorney Maximilien de Robespierre (1758-1794).[49] During the Reign of Terror, the number of people executed after a trial was around 17,000, with an additional 30,000-40,000 executions without a trial.[50] In the last months of the Reign of Terror the rate of people being guillotined in Paris alone was thirty per day.[51] Besides the guillotine, other efficient methods of killing people were devised including mass executions before canon fire and mass drowning, where boats crammed with people would be sunk, and then refloated in order to add more people for drowning.[52]

Practicing Catholics made up many of the state's victims. The French state also directed its hatred towards Catholicism by destroying Catholic signs. Confessionals, altars, statues, and crosses were destroyed, and precious metals from these Catholic symbols were melted down to in-

---

[48] Cronin, *Louis and Antoinette*, 13.

[49] Peter McPhee, *Robespierre, A Revolutionary Life* (Cornwall: Yale University Press, 2012), 22.

[50] Paul R. Hanson, *Contesting the French Revolution* (Oxford: Wiley-Blackwell, 2009), 173.

[51] Hanson, *Contesting the French Revolution*, 173.

[52] Hanson, *Contesting the French Revolution*, 175; John Marsh, *The Liberal Delusion: The Roots of Our Current Moral Crisis* (St. Edmunds: Arena Books, 2012), 134.

crease the state's financial holdings.

Near the end of the Reign of Terror, on July 17, 1794, the state publicly guillotined sixteen members of the Carmelite convent of Compiegne on the charge of keeping a convent open.[53] In their convent these sisters, who have since been beatified, had been daily offering themselves to God so that peace would be restored to France and the Reign of Terror would end.[54] As they walked to be guillotined they prayed out loud the *Salve Regina*, and Psalm 117 *Laudate Dominum Omnes Gentes* (Praise the Lord all People).[55] Their executions helped to awaken the consciences of many French people. A few weeks after their deaths, the architect of death, Robespierre, was executed on orders of the Convention, signaling an end to the Reign of Terror.[56] Those who ordered Robespierre to be executed then set about forming a new government, the Directory.

### 4. The Directory (1795-1799)

The Directory consisted of five men who shared in ex-

---

[53] William Bush, *To Quell the Terror: The True Story of the Carmelite Martyrs of Compiegne* (Washington, DC: ICS Publications, 1999), xxii-xxiii.

[54] Bush, *To Quell the Terror*, 6.

[55] Bush, *To Quell the Terror*, 14-15.

[56] McPhee, *Robespierre, A Revolutionary Life*, 220, 242.

ecutive power so as to prevent one man, like Robespierre, from concentrating all power in himself. Under the Directory's rule, anti-Catholic persecution continued but in a more subdued manner. One notable exception was the War in the Vendee that had begun under the time of the National Convention and was concluded under the Directory. Contrary to the state's anti-Catholic legislation, the predominantly Catholic population of Vendee had insisted on openly practicing Catholicism. During the French government's crackdown of this civil disobedience, around 200,000 people died.[57]

**Romanticism**

The art that accompanied the revolutionary sentiment of this era is known as Romanticism. Romantic art was a reaction to the Enlightenment's emphasis on reason, law, and exact scientific reasoning. According to many artists, what had been ignored by many Enlightenment thinkers were human emotions. They, therefore, began creating a new form of art that exalted emotion, spontaneity, the awesome forces of nature, dreams, love, and even the once

---

[57] Hugh Gough, *The Terror in the French Revolution*, Second Edition (New York: Palgrave MacMillan, 2010), 2, 43; George James Hill, *The Story of the War in La Vend'ee: and the Little Chouannerie* (New York: D. & J. Sadlier & Co. 1885), vii-viii.

overlooked reality in art of insanity and tragedy.[58] In accordance with Rousseau, the philosopher of the French Revolution, the Romantics believed, explains Janson, "that evil would disappear if people were only to behave 'naturally' and give their impulses free reign."[59]

Romanticism was expressed in a variety of artistic media. In music, the son of J.S. Bach, C.P.E. Bach (1714-1788), embraced this style. C.P.E. Bach is not only representative of early musical Romanticism but also represents a shift in how art was appreciated. The new art of C.P.E. Bach's time was composed to express the interior emotions of the artist with the hope that those who heard it, primarily the new middle-class, would identify with the emotions and buy the music. In contrast, traditional music as represented by J.S. Bach who composed all his music for the greater glory of God was directed to God and rulers who represented His authority.[60]

By 1770, C.P.E. Bach had successfully marketed his art by mail. His approaching his art as a commodity on the

---

[58] H.W. Janson, and Anthony F. Janson, *History of Art*, sixth ed. (New York: Harry N. Abrams, 2001), 658; William Kloss, *A History of European Art* (Chantilly: The Great Courses, 2005), 255-260.

[59] Janson and Janson, *History of Art*, sixth ed., 658.

[60] Jonathan Steinberg, *European History and European Lives: 1715 to 1914*, CDs and Course Guidebook (Chantilly: Great Courses, 2003), 59.

market place significantly differed from his father's approach. His father, a devout Lutheran, was concerned with representing the truth of God so as to bring people to worship. One way that J.S. Bach did this was by incorporating mathematical truth, such as the Fibonacci series, into his compositions. His son and others distanced themselves from this manner of composing by developing a theory of emotions, called The Doctrine of the Emotions.[61]

A few expressions of Romantic art in painting are presented on the following pages:

---

[61] Steinberg, *European History and European Lives: 1715 to 1914*, 61.

## J. M. W. Turner (1775 –1851)

Turner was an English Romantic artist. Below are two of his paintings: *Rain, Steam and Speed* and *The Burning of the Houses of Lords and Commons*.

62

---

[62] http://www.artrenewal.org/pages/artwork.php?artworkid=14508&size=huge, "Rain, Steam and Speed [by Joseph M.W. Turner] - The Great Western Railway; the painting depicts an early locomotive of the Great Western Railway crossing the River Thames on Brunel's recently completed Maidenhead Railway Bridge. The painting is also credited for allowing a glimpse of the Romantic strife within Turner and his contemporaries over the issue of the technological advancement during the Industrial

Chapter 3 Politics and Revolution                                      75

63

Revolution." http://commons.wikimedia.org/wiki/File%3ARain_Steam_and_Speed_the_Great_Western_Railway.jpg.

[63] 29 November 2004 (original upload date) on the English Wikipedia, by Solipsist, "The Burning of the Houses of Lords and Commons, 16th October, 1834, by J.M.W Turner. Turner witnessed the fire that burnt down most of the Palace of Westminster on 16 October 1834. He made a watercolour sketch at the time, which he then used as the basis of several larger paintings. As well as this one, he also painted a more distant view with the same title (now at the Cleveland Museum of Art) and The Burning of the Houses of Parliament (Tate Gallery)," http://commons.wikimedia.org/wiki/File%3ATurner-The_Burning_of_the_Houses_of_Lords_and_Commons.jpg.

*John Constable (1776 –1837)*

John Constable was also an English Romantic artist. Below is his painting *The Hay Wain*.

*Thomas Gainsborough (1727-1788)*

Thomas Gainsborough was yet another English portrait artist. I have included this painting because of how well he captured the tender expression on Mrs. Richard Brinsley Sheridan's face.

---

[64] John Constable, "The Hay Wain," painting, http://commons.wikimedia.org/wiki/File%3AJohn_Constable_The_Hay_Wain.jpg.

Chapter 3 Politics and Revolution 77

65

⁶⁵ National Gallery of Art Open Access Images Project, "Portrait of Mrs Richard Brinsley Sheridan by Thomas Gainsborough," painting, http://commons.wikimedia.org/wiki/File%3A Thomas_Gainsborough__Mrs._Richard_Brinsley_Sheridan_.jpg.

*Caspar David Friedrich (1774-1840)*

Casper David Friedrich was a Romantic artist from Germany. Notice how the man in the painting *The Wanderer above the Sea of Fog* is contemplating the uncontrollable forces of nature.

[66] The photographic reproduction was done by Cybershot800i, "The Wanderer above the Sea of Fog by Caspar David Friedrich," http://commons.wikimedia.org/wiki/File%3A Caspar_David_Friedrich__Wanderer_above_the_sea_of_fog.jpg.

Chapter 3 Politics and Revolution

*Thomas Cole (1801-1848)*

Thomas Cole was an American Romantic artist. Below, in his *The Oxbow* we see the Connecticut River, to the right, and a passing thunderstorm, to the left.

67

---

[67] "*View from Mount Holyoke, Northampton, MA, after a Thunderstorm—The Oxbow* by Thomas Cole," http:// commons.wikimedia.org/wiki/File%3ACole_Thomas_The_Oxbow_(The_Connecticut_River_near_Northampton_1836).jpg.

*Albert Bierstadt (1830 –1902)*

Albert Bierstadt was a German-American Romantic painter. Below is his painting Yosemite Valley, situated in central California.

---

[68] forum.netfotograf.com, "Yosemite Valley by Albert Bierdstadt," painting, http://commons.wikimedia.org/wiki/File%3ABierstadt_Albert_Yosemite_Valley_Yellowstone_Park.jpg.

Chapter 3 Politics and Revolution          81

*Frederic Edwin Church (1826-1900)*

The American Frederic Edwin Church also painted beautiful landscapes. Below is a painting of his on New York's and Canada's Niagara Falls.

69

---

[69] The Bridgeman Art Library, Object 445386, "Niagara Falls by Frederic Edwin Church," painting, http://commons. wikimedia.org/wiki/File:Frederic_Edwin_Church_-_Niagara_Falls_-_WGA04867.jpg.

## Anne-Louis Trioson (1767-1824)

Anne-Louis Trioson was a French Romantic painter. Her painting *The Funeral of Atala* depicts passionate love at a funeral.

---

[70] "The Funeral of Atala (The Entombment of Atala), 'Por la corrección y la elegancia del dibujo, este lienzo recuerda las tendencias de la escuela de David, pero devuelve también el efecto romántico que Chateaubriand, de regreso de las orillas del Ontario y del Meschacébé, había inaugurado en la literatura.',״ painting, http://commons.wikimedia.org/wiki/File%3AAtala_au_tombeau%2C1808%2CGirodet_de_Roussy_-Trioson%2C_Louvre..JPG.

Chapter 3 Politics and Revolution 83

*Henry Fuseli (1741-1824)*

Henry Fuseli was a Swiss Romantic painter. The painting below is on an irrational nightmare.

*William Blake (1757-1827)*

William Blake was an English Romantic poet and painter. Below, is a painting of his based on the Book of

---

[71] wartburg.edu, "The Nightmare by Henry Fuseli," painting, http://commons.wikimedia.org/wiki/File%3AJohn_Henry_Fuseli_-_The_Nightmare.JPG.

Revelation, chapter twelve. The painting is entitled *The Great Red Dragon and the Woman Clothed with Sun.*

---

[72] The Yorck Project: 10.000 Meisterwerke der Malerei. Dvd-Rom, 2002. ISBN 3936122202. Distributed by DIRECTMEDIA Publishing GmbH, "El gran dragón rojo y la mujer vestida de sol by William Blake," painting, http://commons.wikimedia.org/wiki/File%3AWilliam_Blake_003.jpg.

## Chapter 3 Politics and Revolution

*Francisco Goya (1746 –1828)*

Francisco Goya was a Spanish Romantic painter. Below is his emotionally-tense painting of the Napoleon-led French army executing Spaniards entitled *The Third of May, 1808*.

73

---

[73] The Prado in Google Earth: Home - 7th level of zoom, JPEG compression quality: Photoshop 8, "The Third of May by Francisco Goya," painting, http://commons.wikimedia.org/wiki/File%3AEl_Tres_de_Mayo%2C_by_Francisco_de_Goya%2C_from_Prado_thin_black_margin.jpg.

*Théodore Géricault (1791-1824)*

Théodore Géricault was a French Romantic painter. The first painting, *The Raft of the Medusa*, is a depiction of an actual tragedy at sea from his times. The second painting is his *Portrait of a Demented Woman.*

---

[74] "Le Radeau de la Méduse by Théodore Géricault, held at the Louvre in Paris," painting, http://commons.wikimedia.org/wiki/File%3ATheodore_Gericault_Raft_of_the_Medusa-1.jpg.

Chapter 3 Politics and Revolution 87

75

---

[75] Rama, "Portrait of a Demented Woman by Theodore Gericault," http://commons.wikimedia.org/wiki/File%3AThe_mad_woman-Theodore_Gericault-MBA_Lyon_B825-IMG_0477.jpg.

### Ferdinand Victor Eugène Delacroix (1798-1863)

We will end this chapter with one last painting by the French Romantic painter Ferdinand Victor Eugène Delacroix. This painting, brimming over with revolutionary sentiment, is entitled *Liberty Leading People*.

76

---

[76] "Liberty Leading People by Eugène Delacroix, 'Romantic history painting. Commemorates the French Revolution of 1830 (July Revolution) on 28 July 1830,'" http://commons.wikimedia.org/wiki/File%3AEug%C3%A8ne_Delacroix_-_La_libert%C3%A9_guidant_le_peuple.jpg.

Chapter 3 Politics and Revolution

## Quiz 3 for Chapter 3

1-5. Compare and contrast the American Revolution with the French Revolution in five ways.

| American Revolution | French Revolution |
|---|---|
| 1. | 1. |
| 2. | 2. |
| 3. | 3. |
| 4. | 4. |
| 5. | 5. |

6-7. Who is commonly considered the philosopher of the American Revolution and why?

    6.

    7.

7-8. Who is commonly considered the philosopher of the French Revolution and why?

    7.

    8.

9-13. Choose one work of art from the Romantic era and do the following.

    9. Name of the artist.

    10. Name of the art.

    11. What the artist is depicting.

12-13. Name two key characteristics of the work that are typically seen in Romantic art.

    12.

    13.

# Chapter 4

## The Rise of Nationalistic Ambitions

**Introduction**

The French Revolution ended when Napoleon Bonaparte, after seizing power, declared himself Emperor of France. His nationalistic ambitions moved him to transform France into an Empire that reached into Russia. Ultimately, he failed, and he died in lonely exile away from his country on the island of Saint Helena.

The nationalistic fervor that he encouraged, though, did not die but rather multiplied and manifested itself in various European countries. The Catholic Prince Klemens Wenzel von Metternich, who had once served as the Foreign Minister of the Holy Roman Empire before it was dissolved by Napoleon, tried to stem the tide of nationalism that he believed was disintegrating Europe and leading to war.

We will conclude this chapter with one style of art that is representative of these times, Impressionism.

## Napoleon's Nationalistic and Imperialistic Ambitions

Before studying the nationalism of France, the term nationalism needs to be defined. In order to understand what nationalism is, the terms nation and state need to be defined.

> A state, in the sense of a politically sovereign state, refers to a defined territory that is ruled by a government that has the power to legislate, enforce, and judge laws. A nation is comprised of a group of people who share significant characteristics. These characteristics may include ethnic, religious, linguistic, and historical components. A nation state is a self-governing political entity that is united by a dominant national identity. According to this definition, not all sovereign states are nation states because it is possible to have multiple nations within a sovereign state. Such a state is a polyglot state and is made up by a number of large national groups. The former Yugoslavia was a polyglot state, which was a factor for its demise. In contrast, the Palestinians are a stateless nation since they have no land of their own and yet are a people. As a further contrast, the Cher-

okee Indian tribe is a nation with land of its own within the U.S.[1]

Nationalism strives to wed a particular nation with a self-governing political entity even if this means breaking from a state that rules the nationality. Nationalism may also refer to a nation-state's attempts to impose its culture over other nationalities and states. During the French Revolution, which we previously studied, nationalistic fervor led the French to war with France's neighboring countries. One key military leader during the French Revolution was Napoleon Bonaparte, who, beginning as a lowly artillery officer, was quickly promoted to the role of supreme Commander of the French military forces.[2]

Napoleon's ambition for leadership did not end with the military. He also wanted to be the supreme political leader of France and even of a French-controlled Europe. To achieve the first end, on November 9, 1799, Napoleon, with the backing of the military, overthrew the French gov-

---

[1] This section comes from my chapter 7 of my *East and South East Asian History* (St. Louis: En Route Books & Media, 2019). For a more detailed explanation of these terms, see Thomas M. Magstadt, *Understanding Politics: Ideas, Institutions and Issues Tenth Edition* (Belmont: Cengage Learning, 2013), 6-9.

[2] Paul Johnson, *Napoleon* (New York: Penguin Books, 2002), 8, 11, 20, 27-28.

ernment and was named First Consul of France.³ A few years later, Napoleon achieved, in part, his second end by crowning himself Emperor of France.⁴ In 1812, his ambitions were curtailed after he invaded Russia in retaliation for Russia's refusal to obey the French Continental System.⁵ The Continental System was directed against England, France's main rival. According to Napoleon's Berlin Decree of November 21ˢᵗ, 1806, European countries that were under the control of France were prohibited from importing goods from England. As article II of the Berlin Decree states, "All commerce and correspondence with the British islands are prohibited."⁶ Since Russia refused to follow this decree, Napoleon invaded.

Although Napoleon won his war with Russia, he in a certain sense lost because so many of his soldiers died during the severe Russian winter. Taking advantage of France's demoralized and weakened military, Russia allied itself with a coalition that included England, Austria, Prussia, and a few other countries. The common goal of the coalition,

---

³ Gregory Fremont-Barnes, *Napoleon Bonaparte* (Oxford: Osprey Publishing, 2010), 13,

⁴ David Nicholls, *Napoleon: A Biographical Companion* (Santa Barbara: ABC-CLIO, 1999), 67-68.

⁵ Nicholls, *Napoleon: A Biographical Companion*, 66.

⁶ Napoleon I, "The Berlin Decree of November 21 1806," Napoleon.org, http://www.napoleon.org/en/reading_room/ articles/files/berlin_decree.asp.

## Chapter 3 Politics and Revolution

named the Sixth Coalition, was to overthrow Napoleon and place someone else on the French throne.[7] The War of the Sixth Coalition with France brought an end to Napoleon's rule.[8] On April 11th, 1814, Napoleon admitted defeat by signing the Treaty of Fontainebleau. According to article one of the Treaty, "His Majesty the Emperor Napoleon renounces, for himself, his successors and descendants as well as for each of the members of his family, all right of sovereignty and domination, as well as over the French Empire and the kingdom of Italy as over all other countries."[9] The Treaty also stipulated that Napoleon would leave France and live in exile on the island of Elba.

With Napoleon safely in exile, the brother of King Louis XVI was named King of France as Louis XVIII.[10] (Remember that Louis XVI and his wife Queen Marie Antoinette were guillotined during the French Revolution. The

---

[7] Rory Muir, *Britain and the Defeat of Napoleon, 1807-1815* (New Haven: Yale University Press, 1996), 220-231, 240, 247, 282-283, 299.

[8] Alan Forrest, *Napoleon: Life, Legacy, and Image: A Biography* (New York: St. Martin's Press, 2011), 263-268.

[9] "Treaty of Fontainebleau, April 11, 1814," Napoleon and Empire Official Text, http://www.napoleon-empire.com/official-texts/treaty-of-fontainebleau-1814.php.

[10] King Louis XVII (1785-1795) was the son of King Louis XVI, and was considered by royalists as the King of France during the French Revolution. He died at age ten.

naming of this brother as the King of France indicates yet another difference between the American Revolution and the French Revolution. Unlike the French Revolution, US Americans never reverted back to being ruled by a King.)

During the turmoil of the French Revolution and during Napoleon's reign, King Louis XVIII (1755-1824), the brother of King Louis XVI, had been in exile for twenty three years in England, a country Napoleon hated.[11] Once backed by the Sixth Coalition and named the French King, Louis XVIII was able to rule France until his death in 1824.[12] For a brief time, though, he lost his power when Napoleon escaped from Elba, returned to France, raised an army, and ruled France for about one hundred days. At the end of the hundred days, Napoleon was defeated by troops loyal to King Louis XVIII in the battle of Waterloo on June 18th, 1815.[13]

Once again, Napoleon was exiled, this time to the island of Saint Helena.[14]

---

[11] George F. Nafziger, *Historical Dictionary of the Napoleonic Era* (Lanham: Scarecrow Press, 2002), 176.

[12] Nafziger, *Historical Dictionary of the Napoleonic Era*, 176.

[13] Nafziger, *Historical Dictionary of the Napoleonic Era*, 1, 55, 75, 249, 301.

[14] John Stevens Cabot Abbott, *The History of Napoleon Bonaparte*, Volume 2 (New York: Harper and Brothers Publishers, 1904), 647.

## German Patriotism and Empire Building

The Lutheran, Prussian politician Otto von Bismarck (1815-1898) successfully helped to navigate Prussia during a war with France from 1870 to 1871.[15] At the conclusion of the war, a common national spirit among various German States was awakened. Building upon this German patriotism that transcended state boundaries, on January 18th, 1871, Bismarck united various German states into a German Empire that shortly was led by him as its Chancellor

---

[15] Bob Whitfield, *Germany, 1848-1914* (Oxford: Heinemann Educational Publishers, 2000), 35-49. For Bismarck's religious views and practices see A.J.P Taylor, *Bismarck The Man and Statesman* (New York: Random House, 1955), 20. Taylor states that Bismarck's "Lutheranism especially never claimed to lay down moral principles for public policy. It taught that service to the state and to the appointed ruler was a high religious duty. Bismarck felt this himself: 'I believe that I am obeying God when I serve the King.' His religion gave to his unstable personality a settled purpose and s sense of power. He said just after Sedan: 'you would not have had such a Chancellor if I had not the wonderful basis of religion.' He believe that he was doing God's work in making Prussia strong and in unifying Germany. The belief itself brought power. God was on his side; therefore he could ignore the opposition of men. Like others who have had this belief, he easily persuaded himself that whatever suited him at the moment was God's purpose…"

and by the King of Prussia as its Kaiser.[16] Prior to the unification, from 1815 to 1866, German lands were part of a German Confederation consisting of thirty-nine states that were relatively autonomous from one another with the Austrian Empire, a predominantly Catholic country and remaining remnant of the former Holy Roman Empire, being the most dominant.[17]

Once he was Chancellor of the German Empire, Bismarck set about unifying his realm even further with his pro-Protestant *Kulturkampf*, which in German means struggle of culture.[18] He believed that only a single Protestant-based culture could effectively unite Germans together as a single empire. Under his leadership of the Prussian *Kulturkampf*, Catholic religious orders were expelled from Prussia,[19] state subsidies to the Catholic Church ended,[20] Catholic seminaries were either closed or strictly regulated

---

[16] Whitfield, *Germany, 1848-1914*, 49.

[17] Whitfield, *Germany, 1848-1914*, 3. The Holy Roman Empire ended in 1806 when it was defeated by Emperor Napoleon.

[18] John Vidmar, *The Catholic Church Through the Ages: A History* (Mahwah: Paulist Press, 2004), 316.

[19] "Anti-Jesuit Law (July 4, 1872)" http://germanhistorydocs.ghi-dc.org/sub_document.cfm? document_id=1837.

[20] Whitfield, *Germany, 1848-1914*, 53.

Chapter 3 Politics and Revolution 99

by the state,[21] Catholic clergy's freedom of speech was greatly curtailed especially from the pulpit,[22] and Catholic bishops and priests were persecuted, imprisoned, or expelled, and decision of appointments of clerics was controlled by the state.[23] Catholics reacted by peacefully forming a Catholic political party called the Center Party whose purpose was to resist further anti-Catholic legislation through parliamentary, democratic means. Their efforts paid off and around the beginning of the nineteenth century when Bismarck, for political reasons, backed off from his anti-Catholic stance.[24]

---

[21] "School Inspection Law of March 11, 1872," http://germanhistorydocs.ghi-dc.org/sub_document.cfm?document_id=670.

[22] "Imperial Law Concerning the Supplement to the Penal Code for the German Reich from December 10, 1871, § 130 of the Penal Code for the German Reich is supplemented by the following § 130 a." "Pulpit Law (December 10, 1871)," http://germanhistorydocs.ghi-dc.org/sub_document.cfm?document_id=669.

[23] Whitfield, *Germany, 1848-1914*, 53.

[24] "Program of the Catholic Center Party's Reichstag Caucus (late March 1871)," http://germanhistorydocs.ghi-dc.org/sub_document.cfm?document_id=683; "Elections to the German Reichstag (1871-1890): A Statistical Overview," http:// germanhistorydocs.ghi-dc.org/sub_document.cfm?document_id=1850; Whitfield, *Germany, 1848-1914*, 54-55.

**Italian Nationalism**

At the time that patriotic fervor was uniting German predominantly Protestant lands, Italian states were also advocating the creation of a single Italy. This trans-state nationalistic fervor also came at the expense of the Catholic Church. Prior to the unification of Italy, Italian lands were divided into the following states: Papal States, Kingdom of Sardinia, Republic of Venice, Republic of Genoa, Grand Duchy of Tuscany, and the Kingdom of Sicily. A 1796 map of these autonomous Italian states is depicted below.

In 1796, the Italian political establishment changed when military forces of the French Revolution, led by Napoleon Bonaparte, invaded Italian states.[25] In 1805, the year following his self-coronation as Emperor of the French, Napoleon was crowned in Milan as the King of Italy.[26] A few years later, in 1809, Napoleon annexed to France the large swath of central Italian lands called the Papal States.[27] When Napoleon lost the war with the Sixth Coalition in 1814, his ambition to establish a vast empire came to an end.

---

[25] Christopher Duggan, *A Concise History of Italy* Second Edition (Cambridge: Cambridge University Press, 2014), xxi, 89.

[26] Duggan, *A Concise History of Italy* Second Edition, xxi.

[27] "Documents upon the Annexations of 1809-1810," http://www.napoleon-series.org/research/government/ diplomatic/c_annexations.html.

## Chapter 3 Politics and Revolution

[28]

---

[28] Capmo (Own work) [GFDL (http://www.gnu.org/copyleft/fdl.html) or CC-BY-SA-3.0 (http://creativecommons.org/licenses/by-sa/3.0/)], via Wikimedia Commons, http://commons.wikimedia.org/wiki/File%3AItaly_1796.png.

After Napoleon's loss, an international political assembly called the Congress of Vienna (1814-1815) attempted to re-establish the Italian states according to the state boundaries of 1796.[29]

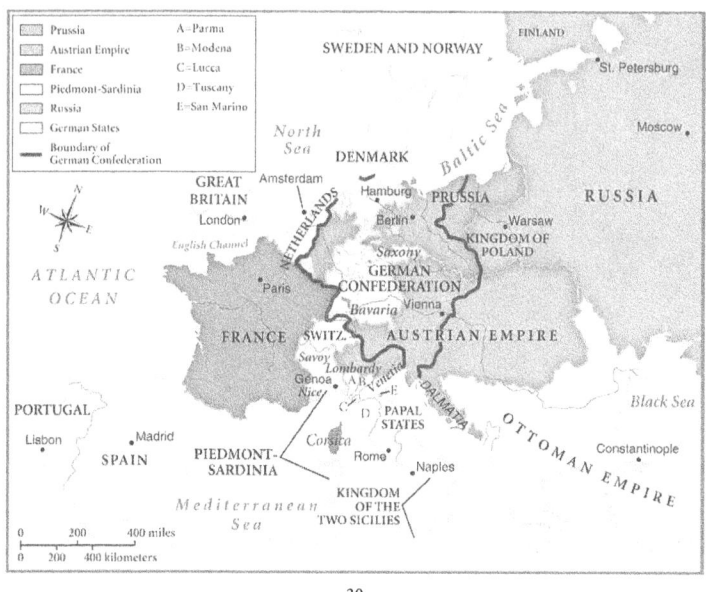

30

The invasion of French troops and their occupation of Italian lands, along with a number of other factors, helped to awaken in some and intensify in others a desire for one united Italy. The principle leaders behind the Italian unification movement were Giuseppe Mazzini (1805-1872),

---

[29] Duggan, *A Concise History of Italy* Second Edition, xxi.

[30] The International Commission and Association on Nobility [Public domain], via Wikimedia Commons, http://commons.wikimedia.org/wiki/File%3AMap_congress_of_vienna.jpg.

Count of Cavour (1810-1861), Giuseppe Garibaldi (1807-1882), and King Victor Emanuel II (1820 –1878). Giuseppe Mazzini promoted Italian unification with his writings and political activism.[31] The Count of Cavour put his leadership role as Prime Minister of the Kingdom of Piedmont-Sardinia, at the service of the unification efforts.[32] The Sardinian King, Victor Emanuel II, also backed the goal of unification with his leadership. Not surprisingly, when Italy did become united, Victor Emanuel II became united Italy's first king. None of these leaders' efforts would have been successful without the backing of military might that General Giuseppe Garibaldi provided. General Garibaldi was also from Sardinian territory, specifically Nice that you can see on the above map. As is evident in the map, the 1814-1815 Congress of Vienna gave Nice to Sardinia.[33]

After a series of battles in 1861, a unified Kingdom of Italy was officially proclaimed with Rome as its capital.[34]

---

[31] George Holmes, *The Oxford Illustrated History of Italy* (Oxford: Oxford University Press, 1997), 188-190, 224

[32] Holmes, *The Oxford Illustrated History of Italy*, 199, 367

[33] Holmes, *The Oxford Illustrated History of Italy*, 189, 194, 196, 201-203; Giuseppe Garibaldi, *The Life of General Garibaldi*, trans. Theodore Dwight (New York: A.S. Barnes and Company1877), 13.

[34] Derek Beales, and Eugenio F. Biagini, *The Risorgimento and the Unification of Italy*, Second Edition (New York: Routledge, 2002), 61-62, 63, 76, 113, 117.

Establishing Rome as the capital was not yet possible, though, since a French Garrison was stationed in 1861 in Rome in order to protect the papacy from the Italian unification movement and to prevent these Italians from seizing Rome.[35]

Circumstances quickly changed when in 1870 the French Garrison was called back to France in order to fight against Bismarck's Prussian forces. Once this occurred, the Italians in support of unification quickly captured Rome on September 20, 1870, and took control over what remained of the Papal States.[36] From that September day, the popes were considered prisoners of the Vatican and remained in this secluded state for fifty-nine years. The self-imposed papal imprisonment came to an end in 1929 with the signing of the Lateran Treaty on February 11th.[37]

The Lateran Treaty established the autonomous Vatican City state that the current pope lives in and rules over today. The signees of the treaty were the Italian Prime Minis-

---

[35] Beales and Biagini, *The Risorgimento and the Unification of Italy*, Second Edition, 155.

[36] Beales and Biagini, *The Risorgimento and the Unification of Italy*, Second Edition, 155-156.

[37] Beales and Biagini, *The Risorgimento and the Unification of Italy*, Second Edition, 3, 118; "Inter Sanctam Sedem et Italiae Regnum Conventiones Initae Die 11 Februarii 1929," Vatican http://www.vatican.va/roman_curia/secretariat_state/archivio/documents/rc_seg-st_19290211_patti-lateranensi_it.html.

ter and Head of Government Benito Mussolini, and the Vatican Cardinal Secretary of State Pietro Cardinal Gasparri, on behalf of Pope Pius XI.[38]

## Austria and Metternich's Anti-Nationalism

In the section on Germany, Bismarck was described as leading the predominantly Protestant Prussian German state to prominence and uniting together a coalition of German states. Prior to the rise of Protestant Prussia, the predominantly Catholic land of Austria had been considered the leader of the relatively autonomous 39 German states. Austria's prominence ended during the Battle of Königgrätz that was at the tail end of the 1866 war of Austria against Prussia.[39] After Prussia once again emerged victorious on January 18th, 1871, in its Franco-Prussian War, Bismarck united Prussian friendly German states into a German Empire in which Austria was excluded.[40]

---

[38] "Inter Sanctam Sedem et Italiae Regnum Conventiones Initae Die 11 Februarii 1929," Vatican http://www.vatican.va/roman_curia/secretariat_state/archivio/documents/rc_seg-st_19290211_patti-lateranensi_it.html.

[39] Gordon A. Craig, *The Battle of Königgrätz* (Philadelphia: University of Pennsylvania Press, 2003), 1-4.

[40] Whitfield, *Germany, 1848-1914*, 49; Mark Willner, Jerry Weiner, and George Hero, *Global History, Volume Two: The In-*

As early as 1819, Austria opposed the nationalistic unification movement spearheaded by Prussia. In 1819, the Austrian Catholic Minister Prince Klemens Wenzel von Metternich issued the Carlsbad Decrees that restricted Austrians from publicly advocating nationalistic unification.[41] Prior to the dissolution of the Holy Roman Empire in 1806 by Napoleon Bonaparte, Metternich had served as an ambassador for the Holy Roman Empire.[42] In the service of this Catholic empire, Metternich came to see the Holy Roman Empire as playing a key role in checking both the interests of small nationalities advocating statehood and trans-state nationality advocating a unification among various states.[43] For this reason, as the Austrian minister Metternich opposed nationalities within Austria (such as, to name a few, Serbs, Croatian, Slovaks, Hungarians) that wanted to be recognized as states. He also opposed both

---

*dustrial Revolution to the Age of Globalization* (Hauppauge: Barrons, 2008), 172.

[41] Willner, Weiner, and Hero, *Global History, Volume Two*, 96.

[42] Clemens Wenzel Lothar Metternich, *Memoirs of Prince Metternich 1773-1835*, Volume One (New York: Charles Scribner's Sons, 1881), 26.

[43] Willner, Weiner, and Hero, *Global History, Volume Two*, 36, 89.

Italian Unification and German Unification efforts.[44] If these micro and macro nationalistic desires remained unchecked, he feared war would result.

One of his first official ways as chair of the Congress of Vienna (1814-1815) where Metternich demonstrated his anti-nationalism was by defending traditional boundaries previously defined by monarchies. Under his leadership, as mentioned briefly before in reference to this Congress, boundaries that were disrupted under Napoleon as Emperor of France were restored. (See previously shown map whose boundaries were established by the Congress of Vienna.) Unknown to Metternich, the main countries and Empires represented at this Congress would later divide into two camps that would eventually fight each other during World War I. The leading countries and empires were the Austrian Empire, its rival state Prussia, Great Britain and the Russian Empire. In November of 1815, these powers reaffirmed their "Quadruple Alliance."[45] After their first meeting in 1818, the four powers agreed to add France,

---

[44] Willner, Weiner, and Hero, *Global History, Volume Two*, 89, 96; Bela Menczer, *Catholic Political Thought 1789-1848* (Notre Dame: University of Notre Dame Press, 1962), 139, https://archive.org/stream/catholicpolitica00menc#page/n11/mode/2up, The Internet Archive.

[45] Jackson J. Spielvogel, *Western Civilization, Volume C: Since 1789* Seventh Edition (Belmont: Wadsworth, 2009), 636.

thereby, forming a five-member alliance.⁴⁶

In time, the common goal of maintaining what has been called a harmonious Concert of Europe was replaced by two rival camps within the alliance. These two camps split to form the Triple Alliance of 1882, and the Entente Powers formed around 1907.⁴⁷ Members of the Triple Alliance were the German Empire (under Prussian Leadership in 1871), the Austro-Hungarian Empire (formed in 1867), and Italy. Members of the Entente Powers were Britain, France, and the Russian Empire. See below.

⁴⁸

---

⁴⁶ Spielvogel, *Western Civilization, Volume C*, 636.

⁴⁷ Spielvogel, *Western Civilization Volume C*, 762.

⁴⁸ Nydas at en.wikipedia (Transferred from en.wikipedia) [Public domain], via Wikimedia Commons, http://commons.wikimedia.org/wiki/File%3ATriple_Alliance.png.

These two rival groups of the Triple Alliance and the Entente Powers set the stage for World War I (1914-1918). In the midst of this tension, the war that broke out brought a decisive end to four empires: Austro-Hungarian, German, Ottoman, and Russian.

**Impressionism**

A number of overlapping artistic movements were present during the rise of European nationalism and unification including, but not limited to, Neo-Classicalism, Romanticism, Realism, Impressionism, and so-called Post-Impressionism and Neo-Impressionism. Since we have already covered Neo-Classicalism and Romanticism, as a kind revolutionary reaction to Neo-Classicalism, we will briefly take a look at Impressionism and its related styles. When we cover the Industrial Revolution in the next chapter, we will examine the art of Realism as an expression of changing social realities brought upon by this factory-based revolution.

A common characteristic of art classified as impressionistic is its blurry quality as if the artists only want to capture what our human mind vaguely processes when given a quick glimpse of something. Perhaps this art appealed to people's sense of their social environment that, due to nationalistic fervor, was in a constant state of flux causing life itself to seem blurry, up in the air, and uncertain. The style named Impressionism came about after the French painter Claude Monet exhibited a painting that, according to some reports, was simply numbered 98. Monet eventually chose to title number 98 *Impression, Sunrise*. The first word of the title was picked up by art critics, and, after much use of the term, a wide variety of paintings from various artists were categorized as impressionistic.[49]

Claude Monet (1840-1926)

Monet's *Impression, Sunrise*

---

[49] William Kloss, *A History of European Art* (Chantilly: The Great Courses, 2005), 274.

[50] "Impression Sunrise by Monet," painting, http://commons.wikimedia.org/wiki/File%3AClaude_Monet%2C_Impression%2C_soleil_levant%2C_1872.jpg.

Chapter 3 Politics and Revolution    111

### Monet's *Waterlilies*

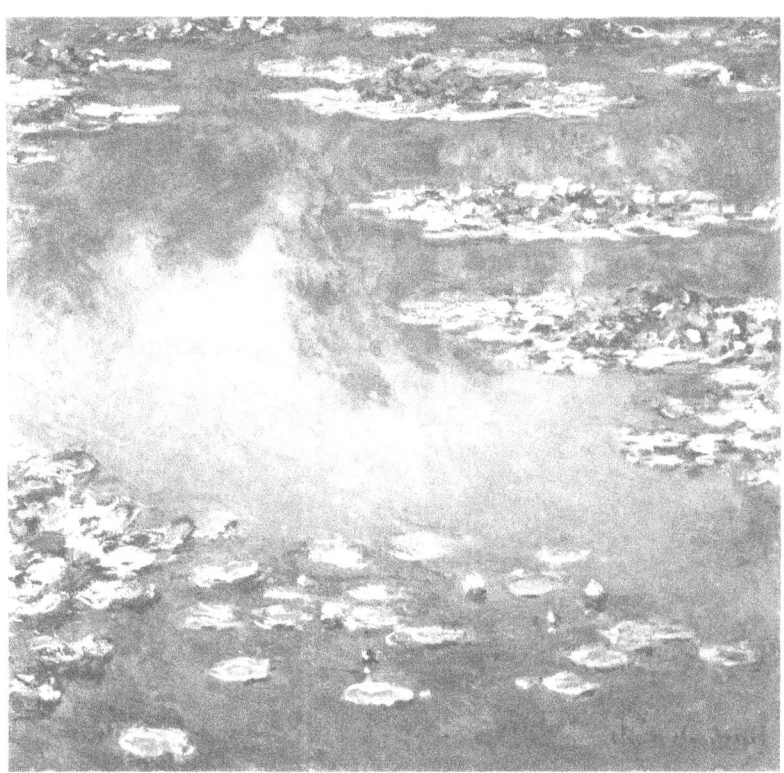

51

---

[51] Repro from art book, "Waterlilies, by Monet," painting, http://commons.wikimedia.org/wiki/File%3AMonet_-_Seerosen_1906.jpg.

## Édouard Manet (1832-1883)

Manet was also a French painter. Some of his paintings have also been classified as impressionistic. Below is his *Blue Venice*.

52

---

⁵² http://www.wikipaintings.org/en/edouard-manet/the-grand-canal-of-venice-blue-venice-1874#supersized-artistPaintings-192160, "The grand canal of Venice (Blue Venice) by Edouard Manet," painting, http://commons.wikimedia.org/wiki/File%3AThe_grand_canal_of_Venice_(Blue_Venice)_-_Edouard_Manet.png. "Manet made this painting during a trip to Venice in 1875. The work is different in

*Camille Pissarro (1830-1903)*

Pissarro was a Danish-French Impressionist artist. Below is his *The Great Flood in Hermitage*.

53

---

mood from his North Atlantic seascapes. Manet had spent time painting alongside Claude Monet that summer and he employed brighter colors and broken brushstrokes to create the visual splendor of Venetian canals. This painting is part of the collections of the Shelburne Museum, Shelburne, Vermont."

[53] Bonhams, "The Great Flood in Hermitage by Pissarro," painting, http://commons.wikimedia.org/wiki/File%3ACamille_Pissarro_(

*Pierre-Auguste Renoir (1841-1919)*

Below are a few impressionistic painting from the French man Renoir. In the first painting, *Luncheon of the Boating Party,* Renoir cleverly unites his painting together with the viewer by leaving the front of the table open as if to invite the viewer to join in the festivities and by interconnecting the painting itself with the various zig zag glances of the subjects complemented by a pattern of similar colors.[54]

French%2C_1830-1903)_Le_grand_noyer_%C3%A0_l'Hermitage.jpg

[54] William Kloss, *A History of European Art* (Chantilly: The Great Courses, 2005), 283.

[55] mgHsTKDNJVzPAg at Google Cultural Institute, "Luncheon of the Boating Party by Renoir," painting, http:// com-

Chapter 3 Politics and Revolution 115

Renoir's *Dance*

56

---

mons.wikimedia.org/wiki/File%3APierre-Auguste_Renoir_-_Luncheon_of_the_Boating_Party_-_Google_Art_Project.jpg.

[56] The Yorck Project: 10.000 Meisterwerke der Malerei. DVD-ROM, 2002. ISBN 3936122202. Distributed by DIRECTMEDIA Publishing GmbH, "Dance at Bougival by Renoir," painting, http://commons.wikimedia.org/wiki/File%3APierre-Auguste_Renoir_146.jpg

*Edgar Degas (1834-1917)*

Degas was a French Impressionist who is particularly well-known for his paintings of dance. By painting ballet as it is practiced behind the scenes and not as it is performed publicly, he created a type of intimacy rarely seen previously in art.

Impressionism is directly related to two other styles that were part of the overall movement of impressionism. Post-impressionism is distinguished from impressionism

---

[57] The Yorck Project: *10.000 Meisterwerke der Malerei.* DVD-ROM, 2002. ISBN 3936122202. Distributed by DIRECTMEDIA Publishing GmbH, "Ballet Rehearsal by Degas," painting, http://commons.wikimedia.org/wiki/File%3AEdgar_Germain_H ilaire_Degas_004.jpg.

not by its placement in time, as is evident in the chart below, but rather by the various distinct ways of expressing impressionism, such as using colors that are not associated with what is being depicted, or, in the case of Seurat, painting with thousands of small points, or using perspective in a unique way.

| Impressionism | Post-Impressionism |
|---|---|
| Claude Monet (1840-1926) | Paul Cézanne 1839-1906 |
| Pierre Auguste Renoir (1841-1919) | Paul Gauguin 1848-1903 |
| Edgar Degas (1834-1917) | Vincent Van Gogh 1853-1890 |
|  | Georges Seurat 1859-1891 He is also categorized as a Neo-Impressionist. |

*Vincent Van Gogh (1853-1890)*

Below are a few works from the Dutch painter Vincent Van Gogh. Notice the emotionally charged nature of his paintings *The Starry Night* and the *Red Vineyard*. It is as if he painted the sky and the vineyard to express his struggle with mental illness which, sadly, ended in suicide.[58] Ac-

---

[58] H.W. Janson, and Anthony F. Janson, *History of Art*, sixth ed. (New York: Harry N. Abrams, 2001), 744.

cording to art historian William Kloss, *The Starry Night* is often understood as a precursor of Expressionism, a style we will cover in another chapter.[59]

60

---

[59] William Kloss, *A History of European Art* (Chantilly: The Great Courses, 2005), 294.

[60] bgEuwDxel93-Pg at Google Cultural Institute, "The Starry Night by Vincent van Gogh," painting, http://commons.wikimedia.org/wiki/File%3AVan_Gogh_-_Starry_Night_-_Google_Art_Project.jpg.

Chapter 3 Politics and Revolution                 119

*The Red Vineyard*

61

---

⁶¹ History of the Red Vineyard by Anna Boch.com, "The Red Vineyard by Vincent van Gogh," painting, http://commons.wikimedia.org/wiki/File%3ARed_vineyards.jpg.

*Paul Gauguin (1848-1903)*

Gauguin was a French artist who has been classified as a Post-Impressionist. He employed a strange, striking use of yellow and red in the painting *The Yellow Christ*.

---

62

http://pintura.aut.org/BU04?Autnum=11164&Empnum=0&Inicio=121, "The Yellow Christ by Paul Gauguin," painting,

Chapter 3 Politics and Revolution 121

*Paul Cézanne (1839-1906)*

The French artist Cézanne has also been categorized as a Post-Impressionist. Notice his unusual use of perspective in *Mont Sainte-Victoire and the Viaducte of the Arc River Valley*. Also, observe how he creates a sense of depth by the denseness of his painting on one side contrasted with an open space on the other, along with one solitary branch reaching out like an arm into the background.[63]

[64]

---

http://commons.wikimedia.org/wiki/File%3AGauguin_Il_Cristo_giallo.jpg.

[63] William Kloss, *A History of European Art* (Chantilly: The Great Courses, 2005), 286.

[64] http://www.metmuseum.org/collections/search-the-collections/110000310, "Mont Sainte-Victoire and the Viaduct of

In *Still Life with Apples and Oranges,* Cézanne cleverly paints still life that contains motion due to placing one, clearly delineated apple in the center with other more hazily painted fruit orbiting around it.[65]

66

---

the Arc River Valley by Paul Cézanne," painting, http://commons.wikimedia.org/wiki/File%3APaul_C%C3%A9zanne_115.jpg.

[65] William Kloss, *A History of European Art* (Chantilly: The Great Courses, 2005), 286-287.

[66] Repro from art book, ""Still life with oranges by Paul Cezanne," painting, http://commons.wikimedia.org/wiki/File%3ACezanne_stilleben_mit_apfelsinnen.jpg.

Chapter 3 Politics and Revolution                                    123

*Georges Seurat (1859-1891)*

The French painter Seurat utilized a technique called Pointillism in his version of Impressionism. His painting below, *A Sunday Afternoon on the Island of La Grande Jatte,* is comprised of thousands of little points of paint. Also, notice his unusual use of a high horizon line.⁶⁷

68

---

⁶⁷ William Kloss, *A History of European Art* (Chantilly: The Great Courses, 2005), 291.

⁶⁸ Art Institute of Chicago, "A Sunday Afternoon on the Island of La Grande Jatte by Georges Seurat," painting, http://commons.wikimedia.org/wiki/File%3AA_Sunday_on_La_ Grande_Jatte%2C_Georges_Seurat%2C_1884.png.

**Quiz 4 for Chapter 4**

1-4. In light of the nations discussed in this chapter, define the following terms: nation, state, nationalism, and imperialism.

    1.

    2.

    3.

    4.

5-14. Compare and contrast in six ways, and in complete sentences, the Prussian politician Bismarck with the Austrian politician Metternich.

# Chapter 3 Politics and Revolution 125

| Bismarck | Metternich |
|---|---|
| 5. | 6. |
| 7. | 8. |
| 9. | 10. |
| 11. | 12. |
| 13. | 14. |

15-17. Choose one work of art from Impressionism and do the following.

    15. Name of the artist.

    16. Name of the art.

    17. What the artist is depicting.

18-19. Name two key characteristics of the work that are typically seen in Impressionistic art.

    18.

    19.

# Chapter 5

# The Industrial Revolution

**Introduction**

We will back track in this chapter to the middle of the 1700s when the so-called Industrial Revolution began in England. Beginning with the invention of the steam engine, we will briefly examine a few inventions from these times, including the creatively efficient manner of organizing labor. For these innovations to occur, a fitting historical context was required. You will be introduced to three ways where the people of these times were historically conditioned to be open to inventing time and labor saving machines and new ways of approaching work. This will be followed by looking at the life of the common worker, in particular children. Finally, we will conclude with how the industrial revolution gave rise to competing political ideologies and led to the gradual elimination of a traditional understanding of a nation's direct relationship to commerce. We will conclude this chapter by admiring first artistic Realism followed by Symbolism that, in part, owe their following to the Industrial Revolution.

## Innovations of the Industrial Revolution

A few of the innovations of the Industrial Revolution were the use of steam power by relying on the steam engine, the use of railways, the use of machine tools, the refined manner of making iron, the replacement of organic wood-based fuels with fossil coal fuel, the use of mechanical seeders in agriculture, the use of water power, the invention of machines that replaced much human labor such as the spinning jenny and the efficient systematization of labor by structuring factory work around assembly lines.[1] The assembly line manner of production was promoted in the US by the automaker Henry Ford. According to his work methodology, each worker is to specialize in a task that he is to perform repeatedly and efficiently with as little movement as possible. See below for Ford's description of this process. Also, below is a picture of the Spinning Mule. This machine enabled the worker to spin cotton and other fibers

---

[1] Steven King, and Geoffrey Timmins, *Making Sense of the Industrial Revolution: English Economy and Society 1700-1850* (Manchester: Manchester University Press, 2001), 13, 49, 55, 51-52, 71, 74-75, 77, 127, 268; Peter N. Stearns, *The Industrial Revolution in World History* Fourth Edition (Boulder: Westview Press, 2013), 6-7, 163; Max Louis Kent, *The British Enlightenment and the spirit of the industrial revolution : the Society for the Encouragement of Arts, Manufactures and Commerce (1754-1815)* (Thesis/Dissertation: ProQuest.umi.com, 2007), 140.

Chapter 5 The Industrial Revolution

into yarn at a very high rate compared to the rate of production of yarn when spun by hand.

Spinning Mule invented in 1779 by Samuel Crompton[2]

3

The US Automaker Henry Ford's description of the assembly line.

> The first step forward in assembly came when we began taking the work to the men instead of the men to the work. We now

---

[2] Gilbert J. French, *The Life and Times of Samuel Crompton* (London: Simpkin, Marshall and Co., 1859), 68, 285, 290.

[3] Pezzab, "The introduction of the Spinning Mule into cotton production processes helped to drastically increase industry consumption of cotton. This example is the only one in existence made by the inventor Samuel Crompton. It can be found in the collection of Bolton Museum and Archive Service.," machine, http://commons.wikimedia.org/wiki/File%3AMule-jenny.jpg.

have two general principles in all operations—that a man shall never have to take more than one step, if possibly it can be avoided, and that no man need ever stoop over.

The principles of assembly are these:

(1) Place the tools and the men in the sequence of the operation so that each component part shall travel the least possible distance while in the process of finishing.

(2) Use work slides or some other form of carrier so that when a workman completes his operation, he drops the part always in the same place—which place must always be the most convenient place to his hand—and if possible have gravity carry the part to the next workman for his operation.

(3) Use sliding assembling lines by which the parts to be assembled are delivered at convenient distances.[4]

---

[4] Henry Ford, "My Life and Work," chapter five, Project Gutenberg, http://gutenberg.org/cache/epub/7213/pg7213.html.

## Causes of the Industrial Revolution

The Christian belief that physical world is reasonable because a divine reason created it helped to provide a fitting historical context during the 1700s that human beings are capable of understanding laws within nature and, hence, in a certain sense, master nature with machines and scientific inventions. Joseph Ratzinger eloquently explains this basic idea of Christianity, inherited by the people of the 1700s, that the world is capable of being understood because it was created by an intelligent being:

> In the ancient and medieval view all being is therefore what has been thought, the thought of the absolute spirit. Conversely, this means that since all being is thought, all being is meaningful, "*logos*", truth. It follows from this traditional view that human thinking is the re-thinking of being itself, re-thinking of the thought which is being itself. Man can re-think the *logos*, the meaning of being, because his own *logos*, his own reason, is logos of the one logos, thought of the original thought, of the creative spirit that

permeates and governs his being.[5]

Another important historical context that helped to set the stage for the Industrial Revolution originated in the practices of Catholic monasteries, which, although suppressed in England by Henry VIII in the 16th century, deeply influenced the psyche of the Renaissance man both in England and in mainland Europe. The clock-work like assembly line that Henry Ford describes has a predecessor in medieval European Benedictine monasteries. As explained in the introduction to Lewis Mumford's book *Technics and Civilization*:

> In Benedictine monasteries of medieval Europe, spiritual and working life was divided into precise units of time, the canonical hours, as a way to magnify the strength of the monks' religious devotion. This regimen gave rise to a need for devices that could measure time: hence the development of the first simple, reliable clocks. The monasteries, in Mumford's view, "helped give human enterprise the regular collective beat and rhythm of the machine; for the clock is not

---

[5] Joseph Ratzinger, *Introduction to Christianity*, trans. J. R. Foster (San Francisco: Ignatius Press, 1990), 31-32.

## Chapter 5 The Industrial Revolution

merely a means of keeping track of hours, but of synchronizing the actions of men."[6]

A third important historical context that, in part, explains the occurrence of the Industrial Revolution during the 1700s comes from Protestantism, specifically the Protestant work ethic. Perhaps unfairly, the German sociologist Max Weber describes this Protestant work ethic, most notable among the Calvinists, as based on the principle that wasting time is:

> the first and in principle the deadliest sins. The span of human life is infinitely short and precious to make sure of one's own election. Loss of time through sociability, idle talk, luxury, even more sleep than is necessary for health, six to at most eight hours, is worthy of absolute moral condemnation…Thus inactive contemplation is also valueless, or even reprehensible if it is at the expense of one's daily work.[7]

---

[6] Lewis Mumford, *Technics and Civilization* (Chicago: University of Chicago Press, 2010), x.

[7] Max Weber, *The Protestant Ethic and the Spirit of Capitalism*, trans. Talcott Parsons (New York: Dover Publications Inc., 2003) 157-158.

In contrast, Catholicism, with its long history of honoring contemplation and people specifically devoting their lives to contemplation, places less accent on the need to work.

**Workers of the Industrial Revolution**

As factories began to be built, machines were invented that replaced traditional forms of human labor, and people not capable of competing with the efficiency of factory production migrated from the countryside to the cities which served as industrialized centers.[8] By 1851, for the first time in England as detailed by Eric J. Hobsbawm, people living in industrialized centers outnumbered those living in the country.[9] By 1881, Hobsbawm estimates, 2/5ths of all the English and Welsh lived in the six major industrial centers of "London, south-east Lancashire, the West Midlands, west Yorkshire, Merseyside and Tyneside."[10] Factory owners found it profitable to hire children from the age of five and upwards since it was customary to pay children significantly lower wages compared to paying adults performing the same work, and children could fit in small spaces and do tasks that required dexterity that few adults could. For

---

[8] Eric J. Hobsbawm, *Industry and Empire: From 1750 to the Present Day* (New York: The New Press, 1999), 21, 135-136.

[9] Hobsbawm, *Industry and Empire*, 135.

[10] Hobsbawm, *Industry and Empire*, 136.

example, children called "Bobbin boys" were employed to tie cotton threads that broke on looms. Children were also hired to drag coal up very narrow mine tunnels. Factory owners wanted child labor so much that they even sought out children from government-owned housing projects, called poorhouses. These child laborers not only received extremely low wages but also were frequently beaten, forced to work long hours without breaks, and were crippled and killed in accidents.[11]

*Young Child Hauling Coal*

---

[11] John Hinshaw, and Peter N. Stearns *Industrialization in the Modern World: From the Industrial Revolution to the Internet,* Volume 1, A-L (Santa Barbara: ABC-CLIO, 2014), 78.

[12] Original uploader was Peaceupnorth at en.wikipedia, "From www.victorianweb.org/history/ashley.html, an educational site offering free info on the Victorian age. Image is a copy of one from an official report of a parliamentary commission done

Naturally, the abuse of children and other injustices led to a growing resentment among factory workers against their employers. The Luddites were a violent expression of this resentment. The Luddites set about destroying the factories that they blamed for causing so much misery in society.[13] Their anger, though, was misplaced since the means of production do not cause misery. Machines are simply means by which owners and workers make products. These means can be used justly or unjustly.

One main reason why there was so much unjust use of workers at factories was because there was practically no safety net for workers to fall back on, nor was there adequate legislation protecting workers from abuse. A possible explanation why these were absent is traceable back to the 1530s and 1540s when Henry VIII was King of England. After declaring himself in 1534 as the head of the Church in England, Henry VIII then set about suppressing thousands of Catholic inspired guilds and dissolved Catholic monasteries. A few centuries later, across the English Channel in France, Catholic guilds and monasteries were similarly

---

in the mid-18th century.," http://commons.wikimedia.org/wiki/File%3ACoaltub.png.

[13] John Hinshaw, and Peter N. Stearns *Industrialization in the Modern World: From the Industrial Revolution to the Internet*, Volume 1, A-L, 288, 644.

abolished during the French Revolution.[14] Up until their suppression and dissolution, Catholic guilds and monasteries provided a social safety net for workers and for the poor to fall back upon.

During the medieval times merchants and artisans united themselves into groups called guilds that had a set hierarchy, ensured quality products were produced, and provided welfare for the members of the guilds and their families.[15] See below for an excerpt from two guilds that detail the Catholic informed welfare these guilds provided for their members.

> Southampton Guild Organization, 14th Century
>
> ...
>
> 7. And when a guildsman dies, all those who are of the gild and are in the city shall attend the service of the dead, and the guildsmen shall bear the body and bring it to the place of burial. And whoever will not do this shall pay according to his oath, two pence, to be

---

[14] Liana Vardi, "The Abolution of the Guilds during the French Revolution" French Historical Studies Vol. 15, No. 4, Autumn, 1988, 704-717; William Doyle, *Oxford History of the French Revolution*, Second Edition (Oxford: Oxford University, 2002), 163.

[15] S.R. Epstein *Guilds, Innovation, and the European Economy, 1400-1800*, (Cambridge: Cambridge University Press, 2008).

given to the poor. And those of the ward where the dead man shall be ought to find a man to watch over the body the night that the dead shall lie in his house. And so long as the service of the dead shall last, that is to say the vigil and the mass, there ought to burn four candles of the gild, each candle of two pounds weight or more, until the body is buried. And these four candles shall remain in the keeping of the steward of the gild.

...

9. And when a guildsman dies, his eldest son or his next heir shall have the seat of his father, or of his uncle, if his father was not a guildsman, and of no other one; and he shall give nothing for his seat. No husband can have a seat in the gild by right of his wife, nor demand a seat by right of his wife's ancestors.

...

22. If any guildsman falls into poverty and has not the wherewithal to live, and is not able to work or to provide for himself, he shall have one mark from the gild to relieve his condition-when the gild shall sit. No one of the gild nor of the franchise shall avow

another's goods for his by which the custom of the city shall be injured. And if any one does so and is convicted, he shall lose the gild and the franchise; and the merchandise so avowed shall be forfeited to the king.[16]

New Regulations: No Work After Sundown
  The Spurriers' Guild of London (1345)[17]

…

In the first place, that no one of the trade of spurriers shall work longer than from the beginning of the day until curfew rings out at the church of St. Sepulcher, without Newgate; by reason that no man can work so neatly by night as by day. And many persons of the said trade, who compass how to practice deception in their work, desire to work by night rather than by day; and then they introduce false iron, and iron that has been cracked, for tin, and also they put gilt on

---

[16] Fordham University, *Medieval Sourcebook: Southampton Guild Organization, 14th Century,* Internet Medieval Source Book, http://www.fordham.edu/halsall/source/guild-sthhmptn.asp.

[17] British History Online. https://www.british-history.ac.uk/no-series/memorials-london-life/pp220-230

false copper, and cracked.

…

By reason thereof it seems unto them that working by night should be put an end to, in order to avoid such false work and such perils; and therefore the mayor and the aldermen do will, by the assent of the good folk of the said trade and for the common profit, that from henceforth such time for working, and such false work made in the trade, shall be forbidden.

…

Also, that no one of the said trade shall take an apprentice for a less term than seven years, and such apprentice shall be enrolled according to the usages of the said city.[18]

Another similar medieval institution were monasteries, principally Benedictine monasteries. According to chapter 53 of St. Benedict's rule, a rule that had a profound impact on the development of Western Civilization, "Let all guests who arrive be received like Christ, for He is going to say, 'I

---

[18] James Harvey Robinson, ed., *Readings in European History: From the Breaking Up of the Roman Empire Volume I* (Boston: Ginn & Company, 1904), 409-411.

came as a guest, and you received Me.'"[19] In accordance with this rule, monasteries welcomed guests hospitably, including poor guests, permitted peasants to farm and graze their lands, and even provided housing for poor students. The presence of monasteries, up until the time of Henry VIII, permitted upward social mobility that without the hospitality of monasteries would not have existed. In other words, by providing lodging to poor students, monasteries enabled these students to rise in social rank. After the dissolution of the monasteries by Henry VIII, however, the gap between social classes widened and opportunities for upward social mobility decreased.[20]

Since Henry VIII in the 1500s repressed these two institutions that each in their own unique manner provided a system of welfare and, in the case of guilds, included legislation that ensured just working conditions, when the Industrial Revolution began in England during the 1700s factory workers, in particular children, lacked protective organizations that could have been in place if Henry VIII had permitted guilds and monasteries to exist and develop. Workers during the Industrial Revolution then naturally began

---

[19] St. Benedict, *St. Benedict's Rule for Monasteries* trans. Leonard J. Doyle (Collegeville: The Liturgical Press, 1948) 72.

[20] Diane Moczar, Seven Lies about Catholic History 1762. Cf. William Cobbett *Rural Rides: in two volumes* (New York: Dutton, 1966).

looking for some type of institution that would ensure they were working in a just environment. They looked towards the anonymous centralized state to provide them with a safety net and began to form unions that were not informed, as the guilds were, by Catholic beliefs and practices.

## Competing Ideologies of the Industrial Revolution

The Industrial Revolution was prepared by and led to a number of competing ideologies. The two main ones were capitalism and socialism. These ideologies explained and responded to the industrial revolution's working conditions, and reliance on child labor in significantly different ways. Eventually, the public dissatisfaction with the working conditions led a number of states to pass legislations that, when enforced, regulated factory working conditions.

### *Mercantilism*

Up until the effects of the Industrial Revolution became prominent in the late 1700s, the dominant economic model was mercantilism. According to the mercantilist theory, economic activities are to be directed by the heads of state, typically monarchs, with the purpose of strengthening the state. For this reason, in the 1400s the Italian explorer, Christopher Columbus, was directly supported by

Spain's King Ferdinand and Queen Isabella with the hope that Columbus's explorations would build up Spain. While this is commonly viewed as an example of mercantilism in action, it is difficult to define what mercantilism actually is. This is because the term mercantilism came into existence not by its supposed proponents but rather by those who opposed an understanding of economics where national leaders protected merchants, and merchants depended on the nation's rulers, principally monarchs. One famous opponent to "mercantilism" was the Scotsman Adam Smith who used this term, in his 1776 *Wealth of Nations*, to describe a state-directed approach to economics.[21]

The following represents a common understanding of the premises underlying mercantilism. (Note well, due to the history of the term mercantilism, the opinion that this term can be defined by a set number of principles has been dismissed by a number of scholars.) The first premise, is that wealth, defined by land, gold, and other hard assets, is quantifiable, material, and hence limited. Wealth, therefore, is increased by taking material assets away from other nations. Ideally, this meant that in order to build up a state,

---

[21] E. Damsgård Hansen, *European Economic History: From Mercantilism to Maastricht and Beyond* (Copenhagen: ADA-Print, 2001), 59; Philip J. Stern, Carl Wennerlind, *Mercantilism Reimagined: Political Economy in Early Modern Britain and its Empire* (Oxford: Oxford University Press, 2014), 3, 12-13.

goods are not to move freely across state lines but rather goods that come from other countries are to be taxed, in order to give a competitive advantage to the home country, and, similarly, goods that are sold in rival countries, or colonies, are not to be taxed by the receiving country.[22]

*Laissez Faire Capitalism or Economic Liberalism*

Adam Smith (1723-1790), in his previously mentioned work *The Wealth of Nations*, proposed an alternative economic system that was beginning to naturally emerge in wake of the Industrial Revolution as the middle class began to emerge. This new economic vision has been named in a variety ways including Laissez-Faire, Free Market Capitalism, and Economic Liberalism. In French, *laissez faire* literally means let them do. As applied to economics, this terminology indicate that it is in the best interest of a nation to let the economic system alone and not interfere with it, which is also why it is called Free Market Capitalism and Economic Liberalism (from the Latin word *liber* meaning free), in the sense of leaving markets alone by not taxing goods that come into a country. As argued by Adam Smith, when a king or nation state leaves the economic market

---

[22] Allen C. Guelzo, Gary W. Gallagher, and Patrick N. Allitt, *The History of the United States*, Lectures 1-36 (Chantilly: The Great Courses, 2003), 112.

alone, the market will naturally adjust itself in a much better way than a political ruler or leaders can. This is so, explains Adam Smith, because the economic market place is ruled by a self-regulating mechanism that he calls, only once in book four, the "invisible hand."[23]

*Socialism*

In reaction to the excesses of the Industrial Revolution and the economic and political theories that were relied upon to rationalize these injustices, such as in a highly competitive world relying on cheap child labor is necessary for economic development, another political ideology developed. It was called socialism. The early socialists, coming from France and England, did not emphasize competition but rather cooperation among people who are essentially social in nature. These early socialists were criticized by later socialists, principally Karl Heinrich Marx and Friedrich Engels, as idealists who lacked a scientific method to implement these noble ideas. Marx, consequently, referred to

---

[23] Adam Smith, *The Wealth of Nations*, Gutenberg Consortia Center, "The Wealth of Nations" http://ebooks.gutenberg.us/Renascence_Editions/wealth/wealth4.html book 4, chapter 2, (Accessed September 9, 2014); Jonathan Steinberg, *European History and European Lives: 1715 to 1914* (Chantilly: The Teaching Company, 2003), 87.

his brand of socialism as scientific since it followed and promoted trends in history that he argued naturally occur.

**Realism**

An art style that can be considered as representative of certain aspects of the Industrial Revolution is Realism. Artistic Realism depicted people in everyday situations even if this included features some would deem as ugly, such as exhausted, sweaty men who are breaking rocks in a quarry on a dismal day. The success of realist art was in part due to a new cliental of art who owed their existence to the Industrial Revolution. Prior to the Industrial Revolution, the patrons of the arts were the few, wealthy, powerful aristocrats working directly for the state. These patrons had a vested interest in supporting only artists who would create works that affirmed the aristocrats' social status.

During the Industrial Revolution, though, a new class of people became prominent, the middle class. Many members of the middle class were merchants, and some even became owners of factories. This new class had a vested interest in downplaying the status of the aristocrats who were born into their social status. One way of achieving this was by supporting artists who were willing to depict in their artwork the reality that the majority of the population experienced and not simply depict the experiences of a few privileged people.²⁴ Below are a few examples of Realist art beginning with the Frenchman Gustave Courbet, who in defending realist art stated, "I cannot paint an angel because I have never seen one."²⁵

*Gustave Courbet (1819-1877)*

*The Stone Breakers*

---

²⁴ Arthurs Efland, *A History of Art Education: Intellectual and Social Currents in Teaching the Visual Arts* (New York: Teachers College Press, 1900), 51.

²⁵ H.W. Janson, and Anthony F. Janson, *History of Art*, sixth ed. (New York: Harry N. Abrams, 2001), 706.

²⁶ The Yorck Project: 10.000 *Meisterwerke der Malerei*. DVD-ROM, 2002. ISBN 3936122202. Distributed by DIRECTMEDIA Publishing GmbH, "*The Stone Breakers* by Gustave Courbet."

Courbet's *Interior of My Studio: A Real Allegory of Seven Years of My Life as a Painter* or *The Artist's Studio* (1854-1855) is shown below. In describing this painting in a letter to a friend, Courbet wrote,

> "I am not yet dead, or realism either, for this is realism…In it are the people who thrive on life and those who thrive on death; it is society at its best, its worst, its average…I am in the center, painting; on the right are the 'shareholders, that is my friends, the workers, the art collectors. On the left the others…the common people, the destitute, the poor, the wealthy, the exploited, the exploiters; those who thrive on death."[27]

Notice the artist, his female model, a small boy, a dog, those in the center admiring his painting. What is more real, the painting of the landscape by the artist, or the people of the painting who are admiring Courbet as he paints?

---

http://commons.wikimedia.org/wiki/File%3AGustave_Courbet_018.jpg.

[27] William Kloss, *A History of European Art* (Chantilly: The Great Courses, 2005), 267.

# Chapter 5 The Industrial Revolution 149

[28] "The Painter's Atelier by Gustave Courbet," painting, http://commons.wikimedia.org/wiki/File%3ACourbet_LAtelier_du_peintre.jpg.

## Jean-François Millet (1814-1875) French Realist Painter

### Millet's *The Sower*

[29] The Yorck Project: 10.000 Meisterwerke der Malerei. DVD-ROM, 2002. ISBN 3936122202. Distributed by DIRECTMEDIA Publishing GmbH, "The Sower by Jean-François Millet," painting, http://commons.wikimedia.org/wiki/File%3AJean-Fran%C3%A7ois_Millet_(II)_013.jpg.

Chapter 5 The Industrial Revolution 151

## Millet's *The Gleaners*

---

[30] CgHjAgexUzNOOw at Google Cultural Institute, "The Gleaners by Jean-François Millet," painting, http://commons.wikimedia.org/wiki/File%3AJean-Fran%C3%A7ois_Millet_-_Gleaners_-_Google_Art_Project_2.jpg.

## Millet's *The Angelus*

---

[31] Google Art Project: Home - pic, "The Angelus by Jean-François Millet," painting, http://commons.wikimedia.org/wiki/File%3AJEAN-FRAN%C3%87OIS_MILLET_-_El_%C3%81ngelus_(Museo_de_Orsay%2C_1857-1859._%C3%93leo_sobre_lienzo%2C_55.5_x_66_cm).jpg. Some maintain that that at least originally this painting was about a couple praying over the coffin of a dead baby.

Chapter 5 The Industrial Revolution 153

*Honoré Daumier (1808-1879) French Printmaker, Painter, and Sculptor*

Daumier's *Ungrateful Country, You Will Not Have My Work*!

---

[32] IgGdwwmVDdcjXg at Google Cultural Institute, "Ingrate patrie, tu n'auras pas mon oeuvre ! (Ungrateful country, you will not have my work!)by Honoré Daumier," lithograph, http://commons.wikimedia.org/wiki/File%3AHonor%C3%A9_Daumier_-_Ingrat_patrie%2C_tu_n'auras_pas_mon_oeuvre!..._-_Google_Art_Project.jpg.

## Daumier's *An Unhappy Young Child Hung on a Wall by His Nurse, Who Has Gone Dancing*

---

[33] http://wellcomeimages.org/indexplus/image/V0011764.html, "An unhappy young child hung on a wall by his nurse, who has gone dancing. Coloured lithograph by H. Daumier, c. 1850.," lithograph, http://commons.wikimedia.org/wiki/File%3AAn_unhappy_young_child_hung_on_a_wall_by_his_nurse%2C_who_has_gone_dancing_Wellcome_V0011764.jpg.

Chapter 5 The Industrial Revolution                155

## Daumier's *A Third-Class Carriage Rue*

This is a depiction of an everyday scene of working class people traveling in a third-class carriage.

34

---

[34] dwGeegIEDB5Fcg at Google Cultural Institute, "The Third-Class Carriage by Honoré Daumier (French, Marseilles 1808–1879 Valmondois)," painting, http://commons.wikimedia.org/wiki/File%3AHonor%C3%A9_Daumier_(French%2C_Marseilles_1808%E2%80%931879_Valmondois)_-_The_Third-Class_Carriage_-_Google_Art_Project.jpg.

## *Winslow Homer (1836-1910) American Painter*

[35] "*The Bathers* by Winslow Homer," wood engraving from a picture by Winslow Homer, published in *Harper's Weekly*, August 2, 1873, http://commons.wikimedia.org/wiki/File%3A Winslow_Homer_-_The_Bathers.jpg.

Chapter 5 The Industrial Revolution 157

## Wilhelm Leibl (1844-1900) German Realist Painter

### Leibl's *Three Women at Church*

36

---

[36] The Yorck Project: 10.000 Meisterwerke der Malerei. DVD-ROM, 2002. ISBN 3936122202. Distributed by DIRECTMEDIA Publishing GmbH, "*Die drei Frauen in der Kirche* by Wilhelm Maria Hubertus Leibl," painting,

158　Western Civilization: Renaissance to Modern Times

**Symbolism**

This late nineteenth century art movement was a reaction to Realism, but it also can be seen as a desire many people felt of escaping from the dreary existence factory life that the Industrial Revolution had helped to foster. In Symbolism, imagination, dreams, and the fantastic are depicted.

*Carlos Schwabe (1866-1926) German Symbolist Painter*

Schwabe's *The Grave Digger*

37

---

[37] Original uploader was H3dg3 at en.wikipedia, "The Death of the Grave Digger by Carlos Schwabe," painting, http://commons.wikimedia.org/wiki/File%3AThe_Death_of_the_Grave_Digger.jpg . "This image might not be in the public do-

## Chapter 5 The Industrial Revolution

*Fernand Khnopff (1858-1921) Belgian Symbolist Painter*

### Khnopff's *The Sphinx*

38

---

main outside of the United States; this especially applies in the countries and areas that do not apply the rule of the shorter term for US works, such as Canada, Mainland China (not Hong Kong or Macao), Germany, Mexico, and Switzerland. The creator and year of publication are essential information and must be provided. See Wikipedia:Public domain and Wikipedia:Copyrights for more details."

[38] The Yorck Project: *10.000 Meisterwerke der Malerei.* DVD-ROM, 2002. ISBN 3936122202. Distributed by DIRECTMEDIA Publishing GmbH, "The Sphinx, or, The Caresses by Fernand Khnopff," painting, http://commons.wikimedia.org/wiki/File%3AFernand_Khnopff_002.jpg.

*Viktor M. Vasnetsov (1848-1926) Russian Painter*

Vasnetsov's *The Flying Carpet*

## Quiz 5 for Chapter 5

1. Name three innovations, except for the assembly line, of the Industrial Revolution.

    1.

    2.

---

[39] belygorod.ru, "*The Flying Carpet*, a depiction of the hero of Russian folklore, Ivan Tsarevich, by Viktor M. Vasnetsov," painting, http://commons.wikimedia.org/wiki/File%3AVasnetsov_samolet.jpg.

Chapter 5 The Industrial Revolution    161

    3.

4. Explain why the assembly line methodology of work advocated by Henry Ford enables a factory to produce more products in shorter period of time and at a lower cost.

5-7. Name and briefly describe three historical causes that helped to bring about a fitting environment for the Industrial Revolution to begin in the West.

    5.

    6.

    7.

8-10. In light of guilds and monasteries, explain how Henry VIII's actions inhibited the development of a social safety net at the time of the Industrial Revolution.

11-13. Distinguish between mercantilism, capitalism, and socialism.

11.


12.


13.


14-18. Choose one work of art from Realism or Symbolism and do the following.

14. Name of the artist.


15. Name of the art.


16. What the artist is depicting.


17-18. Name two key characteristics of the work that are typically seen in art of Realism or Symbolism.

17.

18.

# Chapter 6

## Imperialism and World War I

**Introduction**

As the Industrial Revolution strengthened already powerful countries, these major world powers began to dominate the resources and markets in less powerful countries.

In examining the Industrial Age of Imperialism, we will focus our attention on Africa and Asia. Then, we will see how in the 1900s the major world empires that promoted imperialistic policies began to crumble and break apart.

In the early twentieth century, World War I (1914-1918) signaled the end four of these empires: the Austro-Hungarian Empire, the German Empire, the Ottoman Empire, and the Russian Empire.

In examining this battle of the empires, we will briefly discuss WWI's causes and victims. This chapter will conclude with a look at some of the art representative of this period, namely Expressionism and Abstract Art.

## Imperialism

Imperialism was the last, and strongest, stage of colonialism that began in the 1500's as major western nations explored unchartered territory. When new lands were discovered, such as the Americas, colonies were established. These colonies were overseen by nations that were often thousands of miles away. During the age of Imperialism, the desire and ability of these powerful western nations to dominate their colonies grew. This growth was a direct result of the establishment of industrialized centers that needed raw materials from other countries in order to produce their products along with the desire of these highly industrialized countries for exotic goods. The rapid growth of colonies during the time of the Industrial Revolution is astonishing. According to William Roger Louis in his study *Ends of British Imperialism: The Scramble for Empire, Suez, and Decolonization*:

> In the last decades of the nineteenth century and until 1914, Europe expanded more rapidly than at any other time. Between 1800 and 1880, the colonial empires added some 6,500,000 square miles to their domains. In the next three decades, the empires grew by another 8,655,000 square miles, extending European sway to over 85 percent of the

world's land surface (up from 65 percent). The British Empire alone extended over one-fourth of the globe and over one-fourth of its population.[1]

**The Conquest of Africa**

One large land mass that European nations scrambled to dominate and control was Africa. From the late 1800s to the beginning of World War I (1914-1918), Africa was divided into thirty colonies and protectorates by competing western nations including Britain, France, Germany, Italy, Portugal, Belgium, and Spain. Below is a map of colonial Africa in 1897. Beneath it is a map that indicates when these lands gained their independence.

Much injustice occurred during the time when Europeans scrambled to divvy up Africa. One territory in particular that was known for tremendous crimes was personally owned by the Belgian King Leopold II (1835-1909). King Leopold privately founded and operated the African Congo Free State. During his rule, the Congolese were treated as

---

[1] William Roger Louis, *Ends of British Imperialism: The Scramble for Empire, Suez, and Decolonization* (New York: Palgrave Macmillan, 2006), 36.

slaves.²

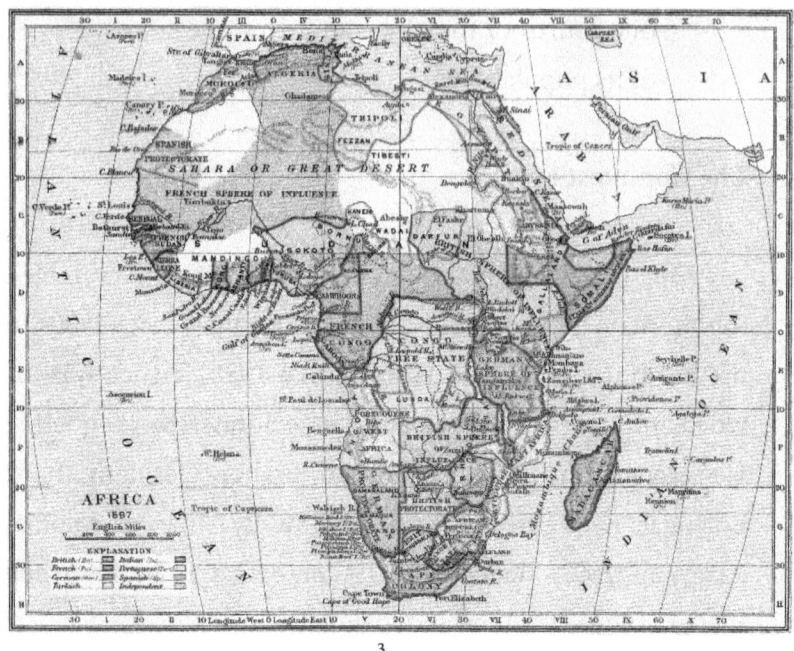

The reason for the abuse was greed. In order for King Leopold and those who worked for him to profit from the Congo's supply of ivory and rubber, millions of Congolese were enslaved. A frequent punishment for slaves who did not collect enough raw material was rape, burning, mutila-

---

² Marie-Bénédicte Dembour, *Recalling the Belgian Congo: Conversations and Introspection* (www.berghahn books.com: Berghahn Books, 2000), 17,18

³ Gardiner's School Atlas of English History, "Map of colonial Africa in 1897," map, http://commons.wikimedia.org/wiki/File%3AMap_of_colonial_Africa_in_1897.jpg.

tion, especially by cutting of hands, and murder.[4]

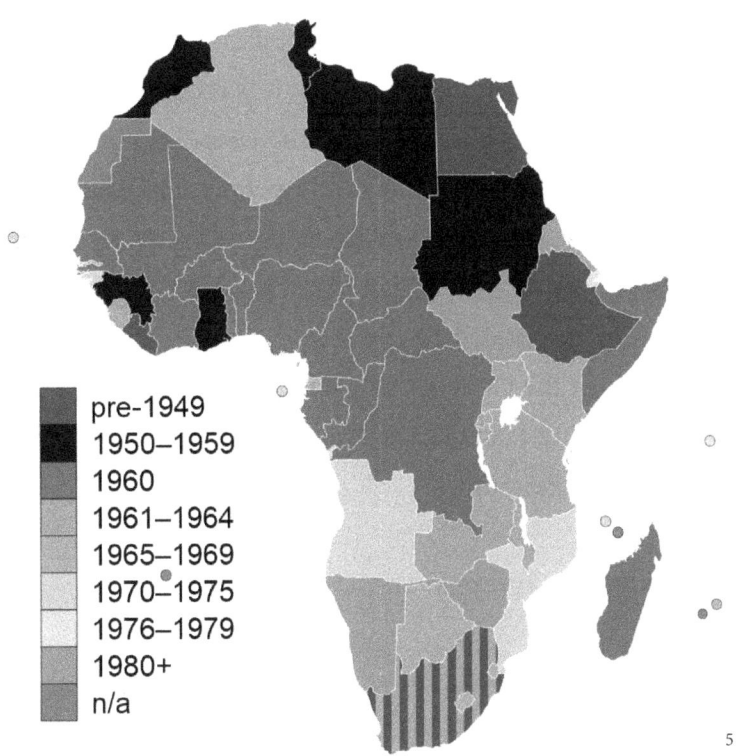

---

[4] Georges Nzongola-Ntalaja, *The Congo: From Leopold to Kabila: A People's History* (New York: St. Martin's Press, 2002), 22. For a photo see http://en.wikipedia.org/wiki/Scramble_for_Africa#mediaviewer/File:MutilatedChildrenFromCongo.jpg.

[5] Original uploader was Mehmetaergun; recreated by Nobelium (talk) 2010-05-10, "Countries of Africa, with date of independence," map, http://commons.wikimedia.org/wiki/File%3AAfrica_independence_dates.svg.

Official census data indicates that as a result of the brutal treatment, the Congolose experienced "a population that was estimated to be between 20 and 30 million people at the beginning of the colonial era, [that] was reduced to 8.5 million in 1911."[6] It is possible that King Leopold was not fully aware of the abuses of Congolese people enslaved to the Belgians since during his twenty-three year reign over Congo he never once visited his territory.[7] In 1908, the people of Belgium responded to the tremendous injustice perpetrated against the Congolese by taking away the Congo Free State from King Leopold and transforming the territory into a colony of Belgium.[8]

**China and the Opium Wars**

Ever since the silk routes that Marco Polo traveled in the thirteenth century, China and Far Eastern countries were associated with exotic goods. The Romans in the first century AD used these routes as attested to by Pliny the elder (23-79 AD) in his *Natural History*.[9] Both the Romans and the British wanted, among other goods, the silk which

---

[6] Nzongola-Ntalaja, *The Congo: From Leopold to Kabila*, 22.

[7] Nzongola-Ntalaja, *The Congo: From Leopold to Kabila*, 23.

[8] Nzongola-Ntalaja, *The Congo: From Leopold to Kabila*, 26.

[9] Xinru Liu, *The Silk Road in World History* (Oxford: Oxford University Press, 2010), 1, 10, 20.

the Chinese were famous for making.

The British were especially intent on controlling China in order to profit by selling Chinese silks, tea, porcelain, and other like goods.[10] The Chinese did not, as a whole, benefit from this economic relationship. This was because part of the economic relationship involved Chinese purchasing and using the addictive British product of opium.[11] When the Chinese government attempted to prevent the British from importing opium into their lands to be sold to the Chinese, the British responded by going to war against the Chinese. These wars are, logically, named the Opium Wars. The First Opium War lasted from 1839 to 1842. This war ended in 1842 with the Treaty of Nanking.[12] According to this treaty, England was to be paid by the Chinese for Opium lost during the conflict, was allowed to trade at Chinese ports, and was able to occupy the island of Hong Kong. Hong Kong was not returned to the Chinese until 1997. The Second Opium War lasted from 1856-1860.[13] This war also ended with a series of treaties that collectively are called the Convention of Peking of 1860. According to

---

[10] W. Travis Hanes III, and Frank Sanello *Opium Wars: The Addiction of One Empire and the Corruption of Another* (Naperville: Sourcebooks Inc., 2002), 12, 15,

[11] Hanes and Sanello *Opium Wars*, 12.

[12] Hanes and Sanello *Opium Wars*, 13, 154.

[13] 3, 175-185.

China's 1860 treaty with Britain, China was required to financially compensate the British for their losses incurred in the war, British ships were permitted to transport Chinese to British Colonies (who would then pay for the journey by working in the colonies), and certain Chinese lands were ceded to the British.[14]

**Imperialist Japan**

During the late 1800s to the early 1900s, many Asian countries became controlled by Western powers. By 1907, the French had taken control over much of Southeast Asia, named French Indochina. The map below depicts the extent of French Imperialism in South East Asia. Today, the territories of Annam, Tonkin, and Cochinchina are part of Vietnam. The map also shows lands that the British controlled.[15]

---

[14] "1860, Beijing Convention – Britain," China's External Relations – A History, http://www.chinaforeignrelations.net/ treaty_beijing.

[15] In 1907, Britain signed a similar treaty called The Anglo-Russian Entente in which Persia (now known as Iran), and Afghanistan were divided between these two Imperial powers. "The Anglo-Russian Entente – 1907," The Avalon Project of Yale Law School's Lillian Goldman Library.

# Chapter 6 Imperialism and World War I

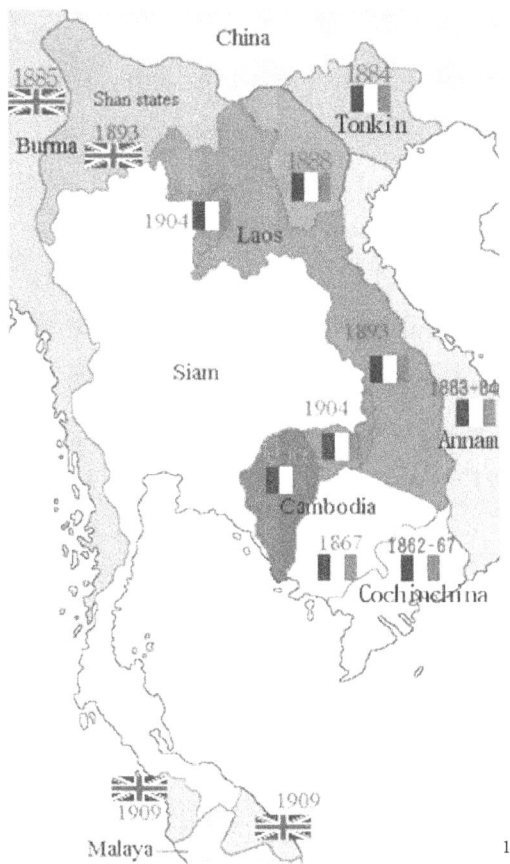

Unlike other Asian countries that became subject to Western Imperialist powers, Japan was able to imitate the Imperialist practices of the West to such an extent that in

---

[16] "French Indochina expansion" by PHGCOM - self-made, adapted from Public Domain. Licensed under CC BY-SA 3.0 via Wikimedia Commons - http://commons.wikimedia.org/wiki/File:French_Indochina_expansion.jpg#mediaviewer/File:French_Indochina_expansion.jpg.

the late 1800s it became an Imperialist Empire itself. Two significant treaties that signaled the entry of Japan into the Western world of commerce were the 1854 Kanagawa Treaty between Commodore Matthew C. Perry of the Unites States Navy and the Tokugawa shogun and the 1858 Treaty of Amity and Commerce between the United States and Japan.[17] Prior to these treaties, and since the 1600s, Japanese ports were closed to foreign vessels. Upon signing the treaties, Japan changed its isolationist policy by opening its ports to the West, beginning with the United States of America. Not only did Japan open its ports to the West but the Japanese also opened their minds to the Western practice of Imperialism.

Soon, Japan began relating to China in a similar way as the British had done during the two Opium wars. In 1895, Japan emerged victorious from a war it fought with China called the First Sino-Japanese War (1894-1895). At the end of the war, China officially recognized the independence of Korea and ceded to Japan the Liaodong Peninsula, Taiwan,

---

[17] "Treaty of Kanagawa English Version," National Archives & Records Administration, http://www.archives.gov/ exhibits/featured_documents/treaty_of_kanagawa/treaty_images.html ; "Treaty of Amity and Commerce Between the United States and Japan, 1858 (The Harris Treaty)," http://core.ecu.edu/hist/ tuckerjo/harris.html.

and the Penghu Islands.[18] This is similar to what China did after it lost to the British during the First Opium War (1839-1842) when Hong Kong was given to the British. Another similarity was after both Britain's Opium Wars with China and Japan's slightly later war with China, China was obligated to pay a substantial reparation fee to Britain and then to Japan. Japan's ability to beat China in war gave Japanese rulers confidence that they could also emerge victorious if they went to war with the Russian Empire. At the end of the Russo-Japanese War (1904-1905) Japan once again emerged as the victor. The Portsmouth Treaty at the end of the war mandated that certain Russian controlled territories in Chinese lands, including the important Port Arthur, be given over to Japan.[19]

**World War I (1914-1918)**

The competing Imperialistic ambitions led to the breakdown of the balance of power that the Congress of

---

[18] "Treaty of Shimonoseki Signed at Shimonoseki 17 April 1895," Taiwan Documents Project, http://taiwandocuments.org/shimonoseki01.htm, (accessed February 1, 2015).

Entered into Force 8 May 1895 by the exchange of the intruments of ratification at Chefoo http://taiwandocuments.org/shimonoseki01.htm

[19] "The Treaty of Portsmouth," http://portsmouth peacetreaty.com/process/peace/TreatyText.pdf.

Vienna of 1815 had intended. Two rival alliances formed out of countries that had, at the time of the Congress of Vienna, committed themselves to unity: the Triple Alliance (the German Empire, the Austro-Hungarian Empire, and Italy) and the Entente Powers (the British Empire, France and the Russian Empire). In 1914, the increasing friction between these two competing alliances ignited into World War I (1914-1918).

At the time of the war, the Triple Alliance became known as the Central Powers, due to the location of the German Empire and Austro-Hungarian Empires and the Entente Powers were named the Allies. At the end of the war, four of the five empires at war came to an end and were dismantled: the Austro-Hungarian Empire, the German Empire, the Ottoman Empire, and the Russian Empire. The fifth, the British Empire, would of its own accord, as influenced by international pressure, dismantle its empire by granting freedom to its former colonies.

The war's immediate cause is traceable to 1908. In 1908, the Austro-Hungarian Empire annexed Bosnia and Herzegovina which it had been occupying since 1878. Prior to the occupation and annexation, Bosnia and Herzegovina had been part of the Islamic, Ottoman Empire.[20] Not only did this annexation irritate the Ottoman Empire that, due to its

---

[20] Margaret MacMillan, *The War that Ended Peace: The Road to 1914*, (New York: Random House, 2013), xxviii, 4, 243.

political and military weakness was called the "Sick Man of Europe," but it also angered the powerful Russian Empire, and Bosnia's and Herzegovina's nearby neighbor, the Kingdom of Serbia.[21]

A few years later, in 1914, the tension between the two military alliances of the Entente Powers and the Central Powers reached a breaking point. On June 28th of 1914, a Serbian nationalist assassinated the Austrian Archduke Franz Ferdinand, heir to the throne of the Austro-Hungarian Empire.[22] In response, the Austro-Hungarian Empire issued an ultimatum to the Kingdom of Serbia. The Kingdom of Serbia reacted by rejecting the ultimatum.[23]

Exactly a month later, on July 28th, 1914, the Austro-Hungarian Empire declared war against Serbia. Soon, all of Europe would be engulfed in a World War that pitted the German Empire, the Austro-Hungarian Empire, and the Ottoman Empire (the Central Powers) against the British Empire, France, and the Empire of Russia (The Allies).[24]

After the German Empire sunk a number of US merchant ships, which Germany believed were directly aiding the Allies, the United States, under President Woodrow Wilson, entered the war on the side of the Allies on April 6,

---

[21] MacMillan, *The War that Ended Peace*, xxviii, 408.

[22] MacMillan, *The War that Ended Peace*, xxvii, 30, 232, 257

[23] MacMillan, *The War that Ended Peace*, 570-571.

[24] MacMillan, *The War that Ended Peace*, 577-580, 637.

1917.²⁵

After millions of combatants and civilians were killed, the war ended on November 11, 1918, Armistice Day. The total number of war casualties is estimated to be around nine and half million men. Fifteen million more men were wounded, and about 9 million others were taken as prisoners of war. These figures do not include millions of civilians who also perished during the war.²⁶ For example, one million innocent Armenian Christian civilians were killed with tacit approval by the Islamic Ottoman Empire, which in 1915 issued the anti-Christian Law of Deportation.²⁷

**Early Twentieth Century Art**

We will now look at art created shortly before and after the turn of the nineteenth century beginning with various styles of Expressionism and ending with styles of Abstraction.

---

²⁵ Byron Farwell, *Over There: The United States in the Great War, 1917-1918* (New York: W.W. Norton & Company, 1999), 35.

²⁶ G.J. Meyer, *A World Undone: The Story of the Great War 1914 to 1918* (New York: Bantam Dell, 2006), 705.

²⁷ The estimate comes from the International Association of Genocide Scholars, http://www.genocidescholars.org/images/Resolution_on_genocides_committed_by_the_Ottoman_Empire.pdf.

**Expressionism**

Unlike Impressionism that, beginning with the material world, captures the artist's first and hazy recognition of objects he perceives, Expressionism first begins with the artist's mind and emotional state through which he interprets what he sees. For this reason, the forms depicted by Expressionism appear distorted, and the use of color by Expressionists can be startling.

The physical reality that is being depicted by these artists was understood as means by which the artist is conveying his emotional state, in other words his inner mood and subjective feelings.[28] Since the artists' political environment was characterized by a high degree of tension that resulted in a world war, it is interesting to note that inner emotional world that artists depict seems often fear- or anxiety-based.

This is very evident in the following two works of early Expressionism.

---

[28] H.W. Janson, and Anthony F. Janson, *History of Art*, sixth ed. (New York: Harry N. Abrams, 2001), 770-778.

178    Western Civilization: Renaissance to Modern Times

*Edvard Munch (1863-1944) Norwegian Expressionist*

*The Scream*

29

---

[29] WebMuseum at ibiblio, "The Scream by Edvard Munch," http://commons.wikimedia.org/wiki/File%3AThe_Scream.jpg.

## Franz Marc (1880-1916) German Expressionist

### Fighting Forms

30

**Fauvism**

Artists of this form of Expressionism displayed their emotional state by even more starkly contrasting colors and by distorting forms to an extreme. The art critic Louis Vauxcelles found this work so disturbing that he called the

---

[30] The Yorck Project: *10.000 Meisterwerke der Malerei.* DVD-ROM, 2002. ISBN 3936122202. Distributed by DIRECTMEDIA Publishing GmbH, "Fighting Forms by Franz Marc," painting, http://commons.wikimedia.org/wiki/File%3AMarc-fighting-forms.jpg.

artists Fauves, which in French means the wild beasts.[31]

*Henri Matisse (1869-1954) French Fauvist*

*Portrait of Madame Matisse* or *The Green Line*

---

[31] Janson and Janson, *History of Art*, sixth ed., 771.

[32] Statens Museum for Kunst, "Portrait of Madame Matisse or The Green Line by Henri Matisse," http://en.wikipedia.org/wiki/File:Matisse_-_Green_Line.jpeg#file . "This image is in the public domain in the United States. In most cases, this means that it was first published prior to January 1, 1923 (see the template documentation for more cases). Other jurisdictions may have other rules, and this image might not be in the public domain outside the United States."

*André Derain (1880 –1954) French Fauvist*
*Charing Cross Bridge*

33

**Die Brücke**

Die Brücke was a German form of Expressionism that, like the Fauvists, used color in odd ways and distorted forms. The emotional intensity captured within these paintings is even greater than works by the Fauvists.[34]

---

[33] "Charing Cross Bridge by André Derain," painting, http://en.wikipedia.org/wiki/File:Derain_CharingCrossBridge.png#mediaviewer/File:Derain_CharingCrossBridge.png.

[34] Janson and Janson, *History of Art*, sixth ed., 773

*Ernst Ludwig Kirchner (1880-1938) German Die Brücke artist*

*Self-portrait as a Sick Person*

---

[35] Rufus46, "Selbstbildnis als Kranker 1918-1 by Ernst Ludwig Kirchner," painting, Licensed under Public Domain via Wikimedia Commons - http://commons.wikimedia.org/wiki/File:Ernst_Ludwig_Kirchner_Selbstbildnis_als_Kranker_1918-1.jpg#mediaviewer/File:Ernst_Ludwig_Kirchner_Selbstbildnis_als_Kranker_1918-1.jpg

Chapter 6 Imperialism and World War I                    183

*Emile Nolde (1867–1956) German Danish Die Brücke artist*

*The Burial*

**Abstraction**

The word abstraction comes from the Latin word to draw, or take away from. In order for me to think in an ab-

---

[36] "Die Grablegung (Begravelsen, The Burial) by Emil Nolde, 1915," painting oil on canvas, http://en.wikipedia.org/wiki/File:Emil_Nolde,_1915,_Die_Grablegung_(Begravelsen,_The_Burial),_oil_on_canvas,_87_x_117_cm,_Stiftung_Nolde,_Seeb%C3%BCll.jpg#mediaviewer/File:Emil_Nolde,_1915,_Die_Grablegung_(Begravelsen,_The_Burial),_oil_on_canvas,_87_x_117_cm,_Stiftung_Nolde,_Seeb%C3%BCll.jpg.

stract manner, consequently, I must strip away materially-based images from my mind in order to think about immaterial concepts. When artists paint in an abstract manner they, likewise, abstract from the physical matter they see in order to depict abstract mathematical shapes.[37] Cubism is an example of early Abstract Art.

**Cubism**

*Georges Braque (1882-1963) French Cubist*

---

[37] Janson and Janson, *History of Art*, sixth ed., 778.

[38] "*Rhum et guitare* (*Rum and Guitar*), by Georges Braque, 1918," painting, oil on canvas, http://en.wikipedia.org/wiki/File:Georges_Braque,_1918,_Rhum_et_guitare,_oil_on_canvas,_60_x_73_cm,_Abell%C3%B3_Collection,_Madrid.jpg, "This im-

Chapter 6 Imperialism and World War I    185

Pablo Picasso (1881– 1973) Spanish Cubist

*Girl with a Mandolin*

age is in the public domain in the United States because it was first published outside the United States prior to January 1, 1923. Other jurisdictions have other rules. Also note that this image may not be in the public domain in the 9th Circuit if it was first published on or after July 1, 1909 in noncompliance with US formalities, unless the author is known to have died in 1944 or earlier (more than 70 years ago) or the work was created in 1894 or earlier (more than 120 years ago.)"

[39] "Girl with a Mandolin (Fanny Tellier) by Pablo Picasso, 1910," painting, oil on canvas, http://en.wikipedia.org/wiki/File: Pablo_Picasso,_1910,_Girl_with_a_Mandolin_(Fanny_Tellier),_ oil_on_canvas,_100.3_x_73.6_cm,_Museum_of_Modern_Art_N ew_York..jpg. "This image is in the public domain in the United

**Futurism**

The abstract art style of Futurism sought to, according to Filippo Tommaso Marinetti's *The Foundation and Manifesto of Futurism*, "glorify the love of danger, the custom of energy, the strength of daring...glorify war...destroy museums, libraries, and fight against moralism, feminism, and all utilitarian cowardice."[40]

*Umberto Boccioni (1882-1916) Italian Futurist*
*Unique Forms of Continuity in Space*

[41]

---

States. In most cases, this means that it was first published prior to January 1, 1923 (see the template documentation for more cases). Other jurisdictions may have other rules, and this image might not be in the public domain outside the United States. See Wikipedia:Public domain and Wikipedia:Copyrights for more details"

[40] Janson and Janson, *History of Art*, sixth ed., 935.

[41] Wmpearl, "'Unique Forms of Continuity in Space', bronze sculpture by Umberto Boccioni, 1913, Museum of Modern Art (New York City)," sculpture, http://commons.wikimedia.org/

Chapter 6 Imperialism and World War I        187

*Angelo de Giudici (1887-1955) Italian Futurist*

*Nice Stranger*

42

**Dada**

The Dada abstract style was a reaction to the systematic, machine-based killings of World War I. The artists who formed themselves into the Dada movement objected to war and, unlike some Futurists, refused to glorify war.[43] Their protest was expressed by nihilism. In their art, they

---

wiki/File%3A'Unique_Forms_of_Continuity_in_Space'%2C_191 3_bronze_by_Umberto_Boccioni.jpg.

[42] Angelo de Giudici, "Nice Stranger by Luigi de Giudici," http://commons.wikimedia.org/wiki/File%3ALa_bella_sconosciu ta.jpg.

[43] Janson and Janson, *History of Art*, sixth ed., 798.

strove to depict life as meaningless by choosing objects that, to most people of the time, rationally does not make sense to be considered as art.

*Marcel Duchamp (1887–1968) French Dada Artist*

*Fountain*

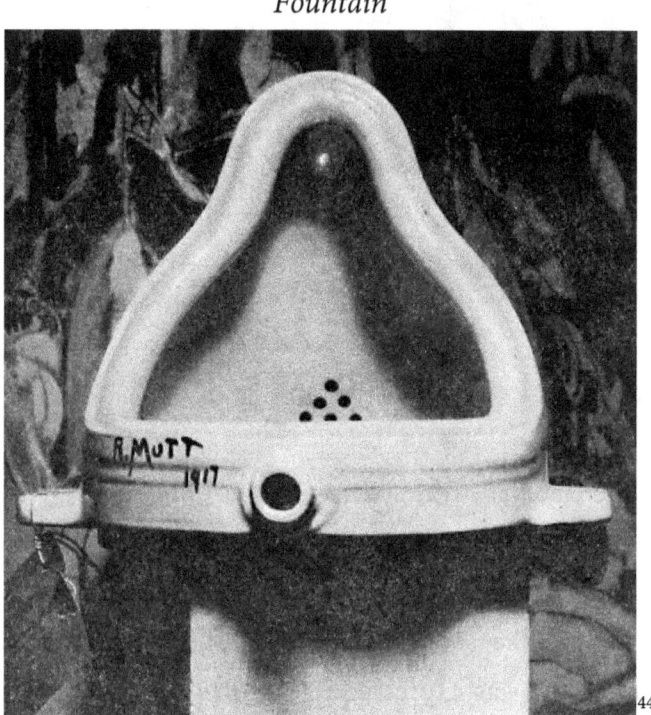

---

[44] src Original picture by Stieglitz, "Urinal 'readymade' signed with joke name; early example of 'Dada' art. A paradigmatic example of found-art. Photograph by Alfred Stieglitz. Captions read: 'Fountain by R. Mutt, Photograph by Alfred Stieglitz,

## De Stijl

The Dutch Piet Mondrian (1872-1944) is known for an abstract style of art called De Stijl, which is characterized not by nihilism but by mathematical rationality evocative of peace. In his painting below, notice that there are no diagonal lines or bars. This is because he associated diagonal lines and bars with violence.[45] In contrast with the immense violent political upheavals around him, Mondrian wanted people to be confronted with peaceful, abstract art.

---

THE EXHIBIT REFUSED BY THE INDEPENDENTS,'" http://commons.wikimedia.org/wiki/File%3ADuchamp_Fountaine.jpg.

[45] William Kloss, *A History of European Art* (Chantilly: The Great Courses, 2005), 315.

## Piet Mondrian (1872-1944)

### Tableau I

---

[46] Gemeentemuseum Den Haag, "Tableau I by Piet Mondriaan, 1921" painting, oil on canvas, http://commons.wikimedia.org/wiki/File%3ATableau_I%2C_by_Piet_Mondriaan.jpg.

# Quiz 6 for Chapter 6

1-5. In light of the Industrial Revolution, explain in five ways King Leopold II's imperialism in the African Congo Free State.

1.

2.

3.

4.

5.


6-10. In light of the Industrial Revolution, explain in five ways Britain's imperialism in China during the time of the Opium wars.

6.

7.

8.

9.

10.

11-13. Describe Japan's relationship to imperialism during the late 1800s and early 1900s. Include in your answer reference to China and Russia.

    11.

    12.

    13.

14. Why is it reasonable to describe World War I as a war that ended empires? Answer this by including reference to the five existing empires before World War I.

15-19. Choose one work of art from either Expressionism or Abstract Art and do the following.

    15. Name of the artist.

16. Name of the art.


17. What the artist is depicting.



18-19. Name two key characteristics of the work that are typically seen in art of Expressionism or Abstract Art.

    18.

    19.

# Chapter 7

# Between World Wars and the Rise of Totalitarianism

**Introduction**

World War I lasted from July 28$^{th}$, 1914, to November 11$^{th}$, 1918. In 1939, it was followed by yet another world war. During the time between these two wars, different versions of totalitarianism became established. The first form of totalitarianism we will examine, including its causes, will be German totalitarianism in the form of National Socialism, also known as Nazism. The second form of totalitarianism we will examine will be Italian in the form of the National Fascist Party. Finally, we will look at Russian totalitarianism that in 1922 became the Soviet Union. This chapter will conclude with Surrealism, an artistic style that began around this time.

**German Totalitarianism**

The German Empire, along with three other empires, ended at the conclusion of World War I in 1918. Once the

German Emperor William II abdicated in November 28th, 1918, as mandated by the Versailles Treaty, his empire was transformed into a democratic republic called the Weimar Republic. The Weimar Republic takes its name after the city where its constitution was written.[1] Although the Versailles treaty brought about greater political freedom, which many Germans were pleased with, its implementation entailed negative economic consequences. The execution of article 231 of the Versailles treaty was at least partly responsible for the dire economic circumstances of rapid inflation that occurred after World War I. Below is an excerpt from the Versailles Treaty, article 231, also known as the War Guilt clause:

> The Allied and Associated Governments affirm and Germany accepts the responsibility of Germany and her allies for causing all the loss and damage to which the Allied and As-

---

[1] Lamar Cecil, *Wilhelm II: Emperor and exile, 1900-1941* Volume II (Chapel Hill: The University of North Carolina Press, 1996), 251, 298, 324; Article 227 of the Versailles Treaty reads, "The Allied and Associated Powers publicly arraign William II of Hohenzollern, formerly German Emperor, for a supreme offence against international morality and the sanctity of treaties." "The Versailles Treaty June 28, 1919: Part VII," The Yale Law School, The Lillian Goldman Law Library, The Avalon Project, http://avalon.law.yale.edu/imt/partvii.asp.

sociated Governments and their nationals have been subjected as a consequence of the war imposed upon them by the aggression of Germany and her allies.[2]

In carrying out the requirement of article 231, Germany admitted it had caused World War I, disarmed, gave up territory, and began to pay a substantial amount of reparation money. Since Germany did not have enough money to meet the reparation payments, it began borrowing money. The combination of borrowing and debt helped to cause, in the 1920s, an unmanageable inflation.[3] In describing the German inflation of the 1920's, Eric D. Weitz writes:

> By the end of November 1923, a single U.S. dollar bought 4.2 trillion marks…Germans carried suitcases and pushed wheelbarrows full of money-to buy a loaf of bread or a pair of shoes. They swarmed over the countryside and railroad yards like biblical gleaners

---

[2] "The Versailles Treaty, article 231" A Multimedia History of World War One, http://www.firstworldwar.com/source/ versailles231-247.htm.

[3] Eric D. Weitz, *Weimar Germany: Promise and Tragedy*, New and Expanded Edition (New Jersey: Princeton University Press, 2007), 38, 91, 1010, 102.

or latter-day thieves, gathering potatoes that had been left behind in the field or coal that had fallen off train cars, or they dismantled fences and took the wood for heating.[4]

In 1931, during the global economic crisis, which began when the stock market crashed in 1929, Germany, with the support of the US President Hoover and the French, ceased paying the war reparation fee and did not resume until after World War II in 1953.[5] Even though Germany was relieved of the requirement to pay its war debt, the inflation encouraged by it deeply affected the German psyche. In times of economic crisis, people often look to a party led by a strong leader to solve their financial woes. The party that matched this description in Germany were the Nazis (National Socialist Party) led by Adolf Hitler.

During the 1920s and 1930s, Hitler and his Nazi party rapidly grew in popularity. In 1932, Hitler had gained so much support among German voters that he became a

---

[4] Eric D. Weitz, *Weimar Germany*, 102.

[5] Theo Balderston, *Economics and Politics in the Weimar Republic* (Cambridge: Cambridge University Press, 2002), 25. David Crossland, "Legacy of Versailles: Germany Closes Book on World War I With Final Reparations Payment," Speigal Online International, September 28th, 2010, http://www.spiegel.de/ international/germany/legacy-of-versailles-germany-closes-book-on-world-war-i-with-final-reparations-payment-a-720156.html.

strong contender in the German presidential elections. Even though Hitler, with 36.8% of the votes, lost the presidency to Paul von Hindenburg, with 53% of the vote, he in a sense won since he had convinced a number of industrialists that he and not Hindenburg could lead Germany to a prosperous future.[6] Acting upon this conviction, these industrialists requested in a formal letter to President Hindenburg to appoint Hitler head of the government.[7]

Heeding their request, Hindenburg appointed Hitler head of the government with the title of chancellor. Not satisfied with this position, Hitler sought for ways to gain even greater power. He found the opportune moment to do so when on 27th of February, 1933, the German parliament building called the Reichstag was burned. Shortly afterwards, Hitler blamed the Communist party for the burning and then banned them. The day after, on February 28th, 1933, the Decree of the Reich President for the Protection of the People and State (AKA Reichstag Fire Decree) was issued. According to article one of this decree:

---

[6] William L. Shirer, *The Rise and Fall of the Third Reich: A History of Nazi Germany* (New York: Simon and Schuster, 2011), 158.

[7] Glasnost–Archiv, "Eingabe der Industriellen an Hindenburg vom November 1932 [Letter of the Industrialists to Hindenburg, November 1932," http://www.glasnost.de/hist/ns/ eingabe.html.

Articles 114, 115, 117, 118, 123, 124, and 153 of the Constitution of the German Reich are suspended until further notice. Thus, restrictions on personal liberty, on the right of free expression of opinion, including freedom of the press, on the right of assembly and the right of association, and violations of the privacy of postal, telegraphic, and telephonic communications, and warrants for house searches, orders for confiscations as well as restrictions on property are permissible beyond the legal limits otherwise prescribed.[8]

Hitler not only supported this anti-civil rights decree, but he also went even further by forcefully insisting that the German parliament pass an Enabling Act, which would give him total power. Out of fear, the Reichstag voted for the Enabling Act and sent the act to President Hindenburg who, by signing it, put the law into effect. The Enabling Act centralized power in Hitler for four years.[9]

---

[8] "Decree of the Reich President for the Protection of the People and State ("Reichstag Fire Decree") (February 28, 1933)," GDHI, http://germanhistorydocs.ghi-dc.org/sub_document.cfm?document_id=2325.

[9] Shirer, *The Rise and Fall of the Third Reich*, 196, 198-200.

To indicate that Germany had entered into a new era, Hitler had the German flag replaced with a Nazi swastika and claimed that under his rule Germany was once again an empire, the Third Reich. The Third Reich, asserted Hitler, was the legitimate successor of both the Holy Roman Empire and the Hohenzollern Empire.[10] When in 1934 President Hindenburg, while still in office, died, Hitler proposed to the German electorate yet another way to consolidate total power in one individual. He requested that the Germans vote to name him both Germany's Leader and Chancellor (*Führer und Reichskanzler*). The German electorate voted in favor of this totalitarian act by almost 90%.[11]

As the leader of Germany, one of Hitler's many horrific totalitarian goals was to ethnically cleanse Europe in order to colonize its lands with Germanic people. As the war progressed, Hitler's desire for Europe to be cleansed from the presence of non-Germanic people and people he considered to be non-desirable became explicit. Included on his cleansing list, but not limited to, were the Jewish people, the

---

[10] In 1871, the Kingdom of Prussia, under the direction of Chancellor Bismarck (ruled as chancellor 1871-1890), unified twenty five German states and the region of Alsace-Lorraine into the Hollenzollen Empire (1871-1919) while excluding Austria. Donald S. Detwiler, *Germany: A Short History* (Carbondale: Southern Illinois University Press, 1999), 132.

[11] Shirer, *The Rise and Fall of the Third Reich*, 229.

Romani (otherwise known as they Gypsies),[12] the mentally ill, homosexuals, Jehovah Witnesses, and Slavic people.

Hitler's military commander, Heinrich Himmler (1900-1945), was the mastermind for executing both Hitler's Final Solution of eliminating all Jewish people and Hitler's massive European ethnic cleansing plan. The so-called Final Solution plan gradually took on greater prominence the longer the Nazis were in power.[13] Its result is called the Shoah by Jewish people and the Holocaust by others. By the

---

[12] Kendall R. Phillips, *Framing Public Memory* (Tuscaloosa: University of Alabama Press, 2004), 210. Quoting from Henry R. Httenback, in "The Romani Porajmos: The Nazi Genocide of Gypsies in Germany and Eastern Europe," in *The Gypsies of Eastern Europe*, ed. David Crowe and John Kolsti (Armonk, NY: M.E. Sharpe, 1991), 31-49, Phillips states, "Given present research data, the total number of Gypsies killed by the Nazi genocidal policy can only be estimated, ranging from a conservative low of 250,000 to a possible high of 500,000, out of an estimated population of 885,000 European Gypsies in 1939. One source claims that 75 percent of Europe's Gypsies were killed by the Nazis, while others, using much higher prewar European Gypsy population estimates, have claimed that 1 million to 4 million died in the Porajmos. Simon Wiesenthal, among others, has stated that up to 80 percent of all Gypsies in Nazi-occupied Europe were exterminated; some scholars feel 70 percent is more accurate."

[13] Gerald Fleming, *Hitler and the Final Solution* (Berkley: University of California Press, 1984), vi-1.

end of World War II, in fulfillment of the Final Solution, six out of nine million European Jews were killed by the Nazis. In two 1943 speeches given in the town hall of Posen, Nazi-occupied Poland, Himmler argued for the extermination of the Jewish People. The excerpt below is from his October 4th, 1943, speech.

**Heinrich Himmler ~ A Very Grave Matter, the Extermination of the Jews**

> I also want to talk to you, quite frankly, on a very grave matter. …I mean the clearing out of the Jews, the extermination of the Jewish race. It's one of those things it is easy to talk about--"The Jewish race is being exterminated," says one party member, "that's quite clear, it's in our program--elimination of the Jews, and we're doing it, exterminating them." … We have taken from them what wealth they had. I have issued a strict order, which SS-Lieutenant General Pohl has carried out, that this wealth should, as a matter of course, be handed over to the Reich without reserve. We have taken none of it for ourselves. Individual men who have lapsed will be punished in accordance with an order I issued at the beginning, which gave this

warning: Whoever takes so much as a mark of it, is a dead man. A number of SS men--there are not very many of them--have fallen short, and they will die, without mercy. We had the moral right, we had the duty to our people, to destroy this people which wanted to destroy us. But we have not the right to enrich ourselves with so much as a fur, a watch, a mark, or a cigarette or anything else. Because we have exterminated a bacterium we do not want, in the end, to be infected by the bacterium and die of it. I will not see so much as a small area of sepsis appear here or gain a hold. Wherever it may form, we will cauterize it. Altogether, however, we can say, that we have fulfilled this most difficult duty for the love of our people. And our spirit, our soul, our character has not suffered injury from it.[14]

Himmler also planned for an even greater cleansing plan in his *Generalplan Ost* (Eastern Master Plan). His 1942

---

[14] U.S. Chief of Counsel for the Prosecution of Axis Criminality, Nazi Conspiracy and Aggression (Washington, D.C.: U.S. Government Printing Office, 1946), vol. 4, doc. no. 1919-PS, 563-564.

## Chapter 7 Between World Wars and the Rise of Totalitarianism

version of this plan specified certain percentages of various European groups who may remain in their territory. Once this cleansing was accomplished, Germans were to immigrate to these lands and populate them.[15] Fortunately, Himmler's plan was never brought into fruition since in 1945 the Allies (led by Britain, the USA, and the USSR) emerged victorious against the Axis powers (led by Germany, Italy and Japan). In the following chapter, we will examine this war more closely.

Below is a prayer in praise of Hitler that is modeled after the Our Father prayer. This prayer was recited by youth in support of Hitler as early as the 1930s.

> Adolf Hitler, you are our great Führer,
> Thy name makes the enemy tremble.
> Thy Third Reich comes, thy will alone is
> Law upon the earth.
> Let us hear daily thy voice and order us by
> Thy leadership, for we will

---

[15] Romuald J. Misiunas, and Rein Taagepera, *The Baltic States, Years of Dependence, 1940-1980* (Berkeley: University of California Press, 1983), 47-48.

obey to the end
And even with our lives.
We praise thee! Heil Hitler!
Führer, my Führer, given me by God,
Protect and preserve my life for long.
You saved Germany in time of need,
I thank you for my daily bread.
Be with me for a long time, do not leave me,
Führer, my Führer, my faith, my light,
Hail to my Führer![16]

---

[16] Jean-Denis G.G. Lepage, *Hitler Youth, 1922-1945: An Illustrated History* (Jefferson: MacFarland & Co., 2009), 87. According to Jean-Denis G.G. Lepage in Hitler Youth, 1922-1945: An Illustrated History, in the 1930s myths about Hitler were created in order to "appeal to the German people's yearning for greatness." Lepage states, "Hitler was depicted to his people as a teetotaler, vegetarian, nonsmoker, and asexual bachelor, as a man without human ties of love and friendship, a man with a divine mission using all his energy and skills for the good of Germany." Jean-Denis G.G. Lepage, *Hitler Youth, 1922-1945: An Illustrated History* (Jefferson: MacFarland & Co., 2009), 87.

**Italian Totalitarianism**

Italian totalitarianism occurred during the same time that the Nazis were gaining power in Germany. It was led by Benito Mussolini (1883-1945) who became the leader of the National Fascist Party and ruled Italy as Prime Minister from 1922 to 1943. Although originally drawn to socialist doctrine and once a party member of socialism, Mussolini split from the Italian socialists to found a party that promoted Italian nationalism.[17] His followers were called *Fasci di Combattimento,* from which the term fascism comes. The full political terminology translates into Bundles of Fight.[18] The Italian word *fasci*, meaning bundles, originates from the Latin word *fascis* which refers to a thick staff of tightly bound sticks with an ax on top that Roman officials called *lictores* used to carry. In public processions, the *lictores* acted like bodyguards for ancient Roman magistrates.[19] Mussolini's fascists acted not only as bodyguards, but also as thugs, specifically those called the Blackshirts, who intimidated those who opposed Mussolini's totalitari-

---

[17] Benito Mussolini, *My Rise and Fall*, Volumes 1-2, (New York: First Da Capo Press, 1998), 17-18, 36-37, 85, 128.

[18] Benito Mussolini, *My Rise and Fall*, Volumes 1-2, 90.

[19] Simonetta Falasca-Zamponi, *Fascist Spectacle: The Aesthetics of Power in Mussolini's Italy* (Berkeley: University of California Press, 1998).

an political vision.[20]

In describing the spirit of fascism Mussolini said it is "a religious conception of life," since fascists form a political "spiritual community."[21] He denied, though, that he advocated, "The crazy idea of founding a new religion of the state or of subordinating to the state the religion professed by all Italians."[22] Even so, he was denying something that he was in reality promoting. His words below indicate that he was advancing a religion of the Italian state, an action forbidden by the First Commandment.

> We have created our myth. The myth is a faith, it is passion. It is not necessary that it shall be a reality. It is a reality by the fact that it is a good, a hope, a faith, that it is courage. Our myth is the Nation, our myth is the greatness of the Nation! And to this myth, to this grandeur, that we wish to translate into a complete reality, we subordinate all the rest.[23]

---

[20] Robert O. Paxton, *The Anatomy of Fascism* (New York: Random House, 2004), 87-91.

[21] Stanley G. Payne, *A History of Fascism, 1914-1945* (Madison: University of Wisconsin Press, 1995), 215.

[22] Payne, *A History of Fascism, 1914-1945*, 215.

[23] From Herman Finer, Mussolini's Italy (1935), p. 218; quoted in Franklin Le Van Baumer, ed., Main Currents of Western Thought (New Haven: Yale University Press, 1978), p.748.

Mussolini's dictatorship of Italy came to a sudden end in 1943 after the Allies successfully invaded Italy. In April of 1945, Mussolini was executed, along with his mistress. Their bodies were then hung upside down in Milan for all to see.[24]

**Russian Totalitarianism**

In 1917, totalitarian Socialism, otherwise known as Communism, became established as the political and economic foundation of the Russian Empire. Pius XI, in his 1931 encyclical *Quadragesimo Anno,* condemned this type of socialism by strongly asserting:

> If Socialism, like all errors, contains some truth (which, moreover, the Supreme Pontiffs have never denied), it is based nevertheless on a theory of human society peculiar to itself and irreconcilable with true Christianity. Religious socialism, Christian socialism, are contradictory terms; no one can be at the same time a good Catholic and a true socialist.[25]

---

[24] Payne, *A History of Fascism, 1914–1945,* 391, 414.
[25] Pius XI, "Quadragesimo Anno," 1931, The Vatican, http://w2.vatican.va/content/pius-xi/en/encyclicals/documents/hf_p-xi_enc_19310515_quadragesimo-anno.html, no. 120.

Prior to the advent of the fundamentally flawed ideology of Communism, Russia had been ruled for hundreds of years by monarchs called Tsars. Public confidence in the ability of the Tsars to effectively rule Russia was seriously eroded when Russia was defeated by the Japanese during the Russo-Japanese War (1904-1905). In response to his people's lack of confidence in his leadership, Tsar Nicholas II abdicated in 1917. He was replaced by a provisional government that was splintered into various factions. One of the political factions that was hoping to rule Russia were the Bolsheviks. In time, the Bolsheviks, under the leadership of Vladimir Lenin, would be called the Communists. The same year the Tsar resigned, Lenin lead the Bolsheviks in a civil war against anti-Communists forces known as the White Army. During the war, the Bolsheviks executed Nicholas II and his immediate family. In 1922, the civil war ended with Lenin and his Bolsheviks as the victors. Lenin then formed the Soviet Union (USSR). Lenin would not see the fruits of his victory, since two year later, in 1924, he died and was replaced by Joseph Stalin.

Stalin wanted the Soviet Union to be at least as industrialized as Western European countries and as the United States. Since building factories costs substantial money, he sought ways to raise capital to rapidly industrialize the Soviet Union within a span of five years. His options were limited since the Soviet Union, in comparison with the countries he envied, lacked a substantial wealthy population that could be effectively taxed. Additionally, the new USSR was not a major exporting nation. What the Soviet Union did have, though, were plenty of farms. In order to raise the needed money to industrialize, Stalin followed a Five Year Plan (1928-1932) during which farming profits were sent to the centralized Communist state. The money obtained was used to build factories. To make this collection of money as efficient as possible, Stalin ordered farms in the USSR to be collectivized and ruled by the state. The means he used to obtain his end of rapid industrialization entailed millions of peasants dying of starvation and millions more being imprisoned or killed during purges that he ordered.[26]

## Art of the Inter-War Period

*Surrealism*

Surrealism aimed at depicting thought of the unconscious mind free from rational restraint. The terminology "unconscious mind" comes from the Austrian psychoanalyst Sigmund Freud (1856-1939). According to a more detailed definition of Surrealism in the Surrealist André Bre-

---

[26] Peter Kenez, *A History of the Soviet Union from the Beginning to the End*, (Cambridge: Cambridge University Press, 2006), 80-103, 132-160.

ton's *First Surrealist Manifesto,* Surrealism is, "Pure psychic automatism by which it is intended to express, either verbally or in writing, the true function of thought. Thought dictated in the absence of all control exerted by reason, and outside all aesthetic or moral preoccupations."[27] The political ideology adopted by Surrealism, before eventually breaking from this allegiance, was Communism. One explanation for this connection was that since Surrealistic artists focused on unconscious drives they were drawn to Communism that supposedly represented the unconscious social drive of people.[28] Due to copyright restrictions, I am not able to show examples of this type of art. Famous Surrealists include Andre Breton, Max Ernst, Rene Magritte and Salvador Dali, whose work may easily be found online.

---

[27] André Breton, "First Surrealist Manifesto, From Le Manifeste du Surréalisme, 1924," http://www.tcf.ua.edu/Classes/ Jbutler/T340/F98/SurrealistManifesto.htm.

[28] David Hopkins, *Dada and Surrealism: A Very Short Introduction* (Oxford: Oxford University Press, 2004), 105. Anna Balakian, and Anna Elizabeth, *Surrealism: The Road to the Absolute* (Chicago: The University of Chicago Press, 1986), 19, 227. Jonathan Paul Eburne, *Surrealism and the Art of Crime* (Ithaca: Cornell University Press, 2008), 168, 244

# Chapter 7 Between World Wars and the Rise of Totalitarianism

## Quiz 7 for Chapter 7

1-3. Explain why the 1919 Treaty of Versailles was partly to blame for the rapid inflation that resulted in Germany's Weimar Republic. (Write a minimum of three sentences.)

4-6. Provide three reasons that explain why Adolf Hitler was able to gain total control over Germany.

5. Besides the Final Solution ethnic cleansing plan of the Nazi's, what was another and similar Nazi ethnic cleansing plan?

6-7. Why or why not was Mussolini's fascism against the First Commandment that prohibits idolatry? (Write a minimum of two sentences.)

8. Briefly state what Pius XI in his 1931 encyclical *Quadragesimo Anno* said about socialism, including "Christian socialism."

9-11. Explain what motivated Joseph Stalin to institute his Five Year Plan (1928-1932). (Write a minimum of three sentences.)

# Chapter 8

## World War II

**Introduction**

After World War I there was a concerted effort to make certain that this war would be the last world war ever to occur. For this reason, the League of Nations was founded in 1919, a year after World War I ended. A main promoter of the League of Nations was the US President Woodrow Wilson (in office 1913-1921). He believed that diplomacy was the most effective policy to prevent the outbreak of war, which is often true, but, as we will see, was not effective when applied to Adolf Hitler, at least not the soft diplomatic tactics Neville Chamberlain attempted. As stated in Wilson's 1918 Fourteen Points, "a general association of nations must be formed under specific covenants for the purpose of affording mutual guarantees of political independence and territorial integrity to great and small states alike."[1]

---

[1] Woodrow Wilson, "President Woodrow Wilson's Fourteen Points 8 January, 1918," Yale Law School, Lilian Goldman Law Library, http://avalon.law.yale.edu/20th_century/wilson14.asp accessed 12/28/2013.

Across the Atlantic Ocean in England, the British Prime Minister Neville Chamberlain adopted a related policy called appeasement. This foreign relations policy, directed towards dictators, was strongly opposed by Winston Churchill. Churchill replaced Chamberlain as Prime Minister when it was evident that the policy of appeasement had failed, resulting in World War II. The war officially ended about a month after two nuclear weapons were dropped in August of 1945 by US manned airplanes on the civilian cities of Nagasaki and Hiroshima, Japan. We will end this chapter with a few works of art whose purpose was to encourage public devotion to the two great dictators of the war, Hitler and Stalin.

**League of Nations**

A peacekeeping league was mandated by the 1919 Treaty of Versailles. The following year, the mandate was fulfilled by the League of Nations' founding. Prior to World War II, its three major Axis powers and belligerents (Germany, Italy, and Japan) all belonged to the League of Nations. Italy and Japan were part of the 1920 forty-two founding nations, and in 1926 Germany became a member state.[2] According to the laws of the League of Nations, all

---

[2] Anique H. M. van Ginneken, *Historical Dictionary of the League of Nations* (Scarecrow Press: Lanham, 2006), 217-218.

member states, including the three just mentioned, were to work collectively in preventing wars from occurring. Interestingly, despite President Woodrow Wilson's commitment to the League of Nations, the US Congress never approved the US to became a member.[3] According to its constitutions, called the Covenant, nations are to:

> to promote international co-operation and to achieve international peace and security by the acceptance of obligations not to resort to war, by the prescription of open, just and honorable relations between nations, by the firm establishment of the understandings of international law as the actual rule of conduct among Governments, and by the maintenance of justice and a scrupulous respect for all treaty obligations in the dealings of organized peoples with one another…[4]

---

[3] H. W. Brands, *Woodrow Wilson: The American Presidents Series: The 28th President, 1913-1921* (New York: Henry Holt and Company, 2003), 216-224; Anique H. M. van Ginneken, *Historical Dictionary of the League of Nations* (Scarecrow Press: Lanham, 2006), 11-21.

[4] "The Covenant of the League of Nations," Yale Law School, The Lillian Goldman Law Library, The Avalon Project, http://avalon.law.yale.edu/20th_century/leagcov.asp.

The outbreak of World War II in 1939 indicated the League of Nations had failed in its peacekeeping mission. A main reason why this league was an ineffective peacekeeper was that it lacked military might. This meant that it was incapable of enforcing peace even if disputes were submitted to it.

**Policy of Appeasement**

As stated in the introduction to this chapter, similar to the US president Woodrow Wilson, the British Prime Minister Neville Chamberlain (1937-1940) strongly believed in the effectiveness of diplomacy. He mistakenly thought that Adolf Hitler could be appeased through diplomatic means. For this reason, the policy he promoted is called the policy of appeasement. Taking advantage of Chamberlain's political naïveté, in October, 1938, Adolf Hitler demanded that regions in Czechoslovakia, called the Sudetenland, which had a German majority, belonged to Germany and not to Czechoslovakia.

Even though Hitler had no legal right to these lands Chamberlain, representing Britain and France, chose to appease Hitler by supporting Hitler's demands.[5] Chamberlain did so by telling the Czechoslovakian president that he had to give these lands to Hitler to maintain peace. Lacking the

---

[5] Antony Beevor, *The Second World War* (New York: Bay Back Books, 2012), 8-9.

support of its allies Britain and France, Czechoslovakia reluctantly gave into Hitler's demands.

*~ Map of Sudetenland in Czechoslovakia According to a 1930 Census ~*

⁶

In assuring people that this was the right decision, Chamberlain said:

> The settlement of the Czechoslovakian problem, which has now been achieved is, in my

---

⁶ Fext, "The percentage of the German population in the judicial districts according to the census of 1930," map, http://commons.wikimedia.org/wiki/File%3ASudetendeutsche.png. "The percentage of the German population in the judicial districts according to the census of 1930."

view, only the prelude to a larger settlement in which all Europe may find peace. (The crowd cheers). This morning I had another talk with the German Chancellor, Herr Hitler, and here is the paper which bears his name upon it as well as mine. (Waves paper to the crowd which responds with loud cheers.) Some of you, perhaps, have already heard what it contains but I would just like to read it to you.[7]

Sadly, instead of guaranteeing peace in the future, Chamberlain's policy of appeasement caused Hitler to be even bolder and gave him precious time to further build up Germany's military strength. In the wake of public disapproval of his appeasement policy that was failing, in 1940 Chamberlain resigned.[8] Winston Churchill then became Britain's Prime Minister and served from 1940 to 1945 and from 1951 to 1955. Churchill had vigorously opposed Chamberlain's appeasement policy. According to Churchill, trying to appease dictators like Hitler was highly risky and placed all of Europe in grave danger of being taken

---

[7] *Neville Chamberlain-Peace in Our Times*, https://youtube.com/watch?v=FO725Hbzfls.

[8] Robert C. Self, *Neville Chamberlain: A Biography*, (Burlington: Ashgate Publishing Company, 2006), 430.

over by Nazi Germany. Churchill held that, "Our difficulties and dangers will not be removed by closing our eyes to them. They will not be removed by mere waiting to see what happens; nor will they be removed by a policy of appeasement."[9] What is your opinion? Do you think that diplomatic, non-violent measures can resolve major world conflicts, including conflicts involving tyrannical dictators?

**World War II**

The beginning of World War II is commonly traced to September 1$^{st}$, 1939, when Germany invaded Poland and France declared war on Germany.[10] Prior to the German invasion of Poland, the Empire of Japan had, since 1937, been at war with China. A year earlier on November 25, 1936 Japan, along with its ally Nazi Germany, signed an anti-communist pact directed against the Soviet Union.[11] This pact was the initial stage of the Axis powers of World War II whose principle actors were Nazi Germany, the Em-

---

[9] Winston Churchill, *Churchill: The Power of Words: His Remarkable Life Recounted Through His Writings and Speeches* (Boston: Da Capo Press, 2012), 373.

[10] Beevor, *The Second World War*, 1, 22, 23.

[11] "Anti-Comintern Pact, German-Japanese Agreement and Supplementary Protocol, Signed at Berlin, November 25, 1936," Yale Law School, Lillian Goldman Law Library, The Avalon Project, http://avalon.law.yale.edu/wwii/tri1.asp.

pire of Japan, and Fascist Italy. After 1939, Japan's Second Sino-Japanese War (1937-1941) became part of World War II led by Nazi Germany. For the first few years of the war the US remained aloof until Hawaii's Pearl Harbor was bombed by Japanese in a surprise attack on December 7, 1941.[12]

The following day, the US, by an act of Congress, entered World War II on the side of the Allies. Prior to Japan's attack, Germany made a substantial military error by overextending its power in invading the Soviet Union, similar to Napoleon's invasion of Russia.[13] Germany did so in accordance with a plan drawn up by Hermann Göring, a leading member of the Nazi Party. Göring wanted food and other resources of the Soviet Union to be directed towards German people even if this meant millions living in the Soviet Union starved to death. His plan, accepted by the Nazis in June of 1941, has been named "The Green Folder."[14]

In June of 1941, another leading Nazi, Heinrich Himmler, estimated, during a meeting with SS Group Leaders, that the population of the Soviet Union would be decreased by 30 million people due to starvation and other

---

[12] Beevor, *The Second World War*, 256.

[13] Beevor, *The Second World War*, 269.

[14] Ulrich Herbert, and Götz Aly, *National Socialist Extermination Policies: Contemporary German Perspectives and Controversies* (New York: Berghahn Books, 2000), 215.

causes encouraged by the Nazis.[15] Heinrich Himmler is famously reputed to have asserted, "I have no conscience. Hitler is my conscience."[16] His willingness to allow and even encourage millions to starve to death is an example of the dangers entailed when someone's conscience is formed only by a political leader and not by laws, reflecting the creator, whom we all are accountable to regardless race. In reference to Himmler's famous saying, Joseph Ratzinger asserts that, "The destruction of conscience is the real prerequisite for totalitarian followers and totalitarian rule."[17] Ratzinger argues that when the authority of conscience is no longer publicly recognized then a totalitarian state will inevitably occur since without a healthy tension between the state and the human conscience the state and its leaders has no check upon itself, nothing to challenge its decisions.[18]

Fortunately, Göring's totalitarian Green Folder plan that Himmler was so eager to implement failed, since by invading the Soviet Union the Nazis had spread themselves to thin. Within a year's time the Allies were able to success-

---

[15] Herbert and Aly, *National Socialist Extermination Policies: Contemporary German Perspectives and Controversies*, 215-216.

[16] John Mueller, *The Remnants of War* (Ithaca: Cornell University Press, 2004), 60.

[17] Joseph Ratzinger, *Church, Ecumenism and Politics* trans. Michael J. Miller(San Francisco: Ignatius Press, 1987), 160.

[18] Ratzinger, *Church, Ecumenism and Politics*, 157.

fully reign in the Axis's drive to control ever more territory. Finally, on May 8th, 1945, Germany surrendered followed by Japan's surrender on August 15th, 1945. Japan's surrender occurred after the US dropped nuclear weapons on the two Japanese cities of Hiroshima and Nagasaki.

**Nazi and Soviet Propaganda**

According to the following Nazi propaganda, "In the occupied regions of the fascist German Wehrmacht areas of the Soviet Union in May 1943 committed young Ukrainian women leave their home by train."[19] In reality, Ukrainian

---

[19] Kurrasch, "ADN-ZB-Archiv II.Weltkrieg 1939-45 In den von der faschistischen deutschen Wehrmacht besetzten Gebieten der Sowjetunion, Mai 1943 Zum Arbeitseinsatz in Deutschland verpflichtete junge Ukrainerinnen verlassen mit der Eisenbahn ihre Heimat. Aufnahme: Kurrasch Scherl Bilderdienst, Freiwillige Ostarbeiter kommen nach Deutschland. Im geschmückten Eisenahnzug und mit frohen, erwartungsvollen Minen verlassen die jungen Ukrainerinnen ihre Heimat, um sich in Deutschlandn durch ihre Arbeit für das siegreiche Gelingen des großen Kampfes einzusetzen. PK: Kurrasch [Mai 1943], 45 In the occupied regions of the fascist German Wehrmacht areas of the Soviet Union in May 1943 committed young Ukrainian women leave their home by train," photograph, http://commons.wikimedia.org/wiki/File%3ABundesarchiv_Bild_183-J10852%2C_Ausl%C3%A4ndische_Arbeiter_im_III._Reich.jpg.

Chapter 8 World War II 225

enthusiasm for the Nazis was minimal since the Nazis, in accordance with Göring's Green Folder plan, were working toward diverting food grown in Ukraine, considered as the bread basket of the Soviet Union, to Germany while deliberately allowing millions of Soviet citizens to die of starvation.[20]

---

[20] Timothy Snyder, and Ray Brandon, *Stalin and Europe: Imitation and Domination, 1928-1953* (Oxford: Oxford University Press, 2014), 9.

[21] Kurrasch, "ADN-ZB-Archiv II.Weltkrieg 1939-45 In den von der faschistischen deutschen Wehrmacht besetzten Gebieten der Sowjetunion, Mai 1943 Zum Arbeitseinsatz in Deutschland verpflichtete junge Ukrainerinnen verlassen mit der Eisenbahn ihre Heimat. Aufnahme: Kurrasch Scherl Bilderdienst, Freiwillige Ostarbeiter kommen nach Deutschland. Im geschmückten

226    Western Civilization: Renaissance to Modern Times

Below, Göring is photographed as joyfully showing the prize he won in a raffle, which appears to be a picture of Hitler.

22

---

Eisenahnzug und mit frohen, erwartungsvollen Minen verlassen die jungen Ukrainerinnen ihre Heimat, um sich in Deutschlandn durch ihre Arbeit für das siegreiche Gelingen des großen Kampfes einzusetzen. PK: Kurrasch [Mai 1943], 45 In the occupied regions of the fascist German Wehrmacht areas of the Soviet Union in May 1943 committed young Ukrainian women leave their home by train," photograph, http://commons.wikimedia.org/wiki/File%3ABundesarchiv_Bild_183-J10852%2C_Ausl%C3%A4ndische_Arbeiter_im_III._Reich.jpg.

[22] "Fest der Deutsch-Oesterreicher im Reich zu Gunsten notleidender Oesterreicher, im Zoo Als Vertreter der Reichsregierung war Ministerpräsident (Hermann Göring) erschienen. UBz.: Der Ministerpräsident verschenkt seine in der Tombola gewonnenen Gewinne," http://commons.wikimedia.org/wiki/

# Chapter 8 World War II

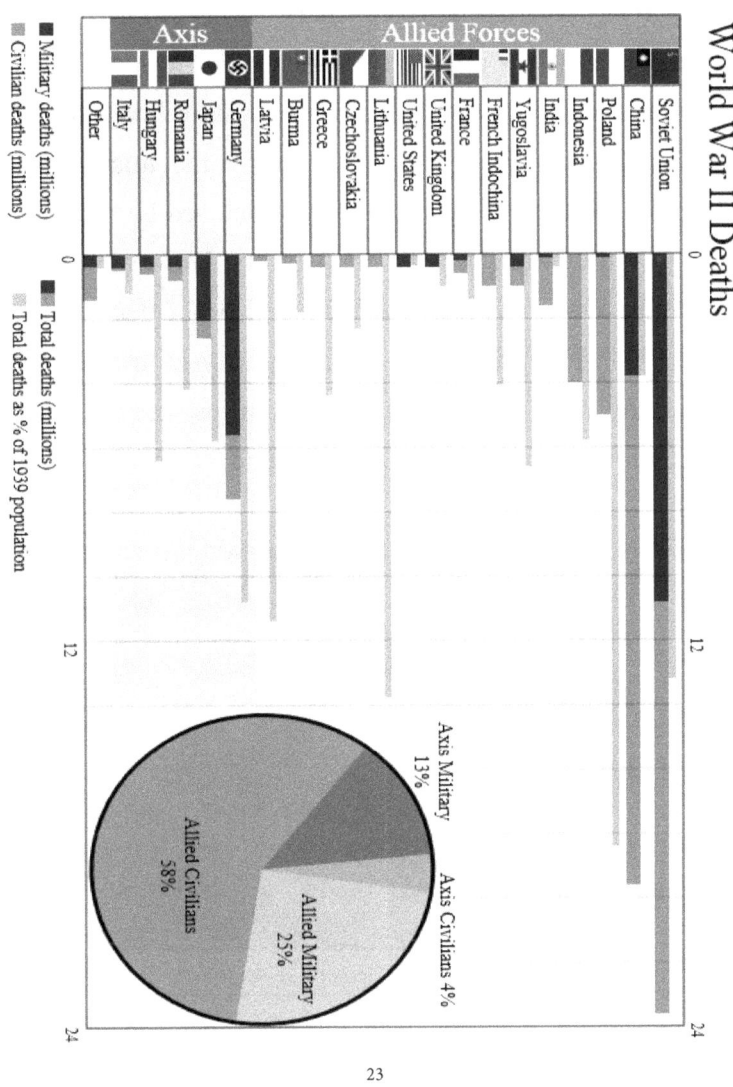

File%3ABundesarchiv_Bild_183-2005-1206-502%2C_Fest_der_Deutsch-%C3%96sterreicher%2C_G%C3%B6ring.jpg.

[23] An image that charts World War II's casualties. Oberiko at English Wikipedia, "World War 2 was devastating for both

During World War II, Germans were bombarded with propaganda of how great their leader Hitler was while Soviets were constantly reminded by their state how magnificent Stalin was. Today, we often make the mistaken assumption that these leaders were not beloved by their people but rather were unpopular dictators. However, at least for Hitler, we have abundant historical proof that sadly, as Klaus P. Fisher points out, "the majority of the German people cheered him on during his triumphs, and they stood by him, for the most part, to the very end."[24]

[25]

the Allied and Axis nations. Five countries suffered the deaths of more than 10% of their population," chart, http://commons.wikimedia.org/wiki/File%3AWorld_War_II_Casualties2.svg.

[24] Klaus P. Fischer, *Hitler and America* (Philadelphia: University of Pennsylvania Press, 2011), 3.

[25] Artwork in the style of 1930's Nazi and Soviet Propaganda that represents the cult of personality that both Hit-

## Quiz 8 for Chapter 8

1. What was the principle reason for which the League of Nations was founded?

2-13. Compare and contrast the following political leaders

| Neville Chamberlain | Woodrow Wilson | Winston Churchill |
|---|---|---|
| 2. | 6. | 10. |
| 3. | 7. | 11. |
| 4. | 8. | 12. |
| 5. | 9. | 13. |

ler and Stalin encouraged. Spiridon Ion Cepleanu, "Derivative drawing according with an idea of Евгений Пивоваров since two posters of the 1930-es, date 3 September 2014," drawings, http://commons.wikimedia.org/wiki/File%3AHitlerStalin.jpg.

14. Why did the policy of appeasement fail?

15-17. Regarding conscience in relationship to Hitler, what reputedly did the leading Nazi Heinrich Himmler say, and why is this assertion of his deeply problematic?

# Chapter 9

## Radical Scientific Discoveries

**Introduction**

In the last chapter, the US dropping of atomic bombs in 1945 on Japan was mentioned. The atomic bomb, named Little Boy, was dropped on August 6$^{th}$, 1945 from an American B-29 bomber over the Japanese city of Hiroshima. It exploded 1,903 feet above Hiroshima instantly killing around 70,000 people and vaporizing much of the city and its people. Since the Japanese government, headed by Emperor Hirohito, refused to surrender, the US dropped yet another atomic bomb, named Fat Man, on August 9$^{th}$, 1945, over the Japanese city of Nagasaki. This bomb also instantly killed around 70,000 people. Finally, on August 15$^{th}$, 1945, Japan officially surrendered.[1] The reason that the US was able to explode this devastating bomb was due to radical scientific discoveries on both the micro level and macro level. This chapter will introduce you to some of these, beginning first with the sub-atomic and biological discoveries

---

[1] Jamie Poolos, *The Atomic Bombings of Hiroshima and Nagasaki* (New York: Chelsea House, 2008), 95-103.

before touching upon some scientific advancements in physics.

[2] Nagasakibomb.jpg: The picture was taken by Charles Levy from one of the B-29 Superfortresses used in the attack, "Atomic Bombing of Japan," photographs, http://commons.wikimedia.org/wiki/File%3AAtomic_bombing_of_Japan.jpg, "Left picture: At the time this photo was made, smoke billowed 20,000 feet above Hiroshima while smoke from the burst of the first atomic bomb had spread over 10,000 feet on the target at the base of the rising column. Six planes of the 509th Composite Group participated in this mission; one to carry the bomb, the Enola Gay, one to take scientific measurements of the blast, The Great Artiste, and the third to take photographs, Necessary Evil. The others flew approximately an hour ahead to act as weather scouts, 08/06/1945. Bad weather would disqualify a target as the scientists insisted on a visual delivery. The primary target was Hiroshima, secondary was Kokura, and tertiary was Nagasaki. Right picture: Atomic bombing of Nagasaki on August 9, 1945, taken by Charles Levy."

Chapter 9 Radical Scientific Discoveries 233

**War and Scientific Progress**

One obvious reason for scientific progress is warfare as the historian A.J. Taylor in his book on World War I clearly asserts, "War has always been the mother of invention."[3] In order to have a technological advantage over their opponents, nations develop scientifically during times of war. This was particularly the case during the two world wars. During World War I, the mobile X-Ray machine was invented, and efficient, effective techniques of infusing blood were created.[4] As M. Anthony Mills and Mark P. Mills explain, "[World War I] functioned like a vast laboratory for the implementation and testing of not only organizational and administrative techniques for medical treatment, but also for the various contagion theories of disease that had been hotly debated in the medical community during the decades preceding the war."[5] Also during this war radio communication and aircraft were greatly improved upon.[6] In 1918, the US Navy even successfully launched and land-

---

[3] A. J. Taylor, *The First World War: An Illustrated History* (New York: Berkley Publishing Group, 1972), front matter.

[4] M. Anthony Mills, and Mark P. Mills "The Invention of the War Machine," *The New Atlantis*, vol. 42 (Spring 2014), 8.

[5] Mills and Mills "The Invention of the War Machine," *The New Atlantis*, 9.

[6] Mills and Mills "The Invention of the War Machine," *The New Atlantis*, 10.

ed a drone.[7]

Like the drone that we now take for granted, which may soon be used commercially, the internet similarly has its origins during the time of the Cold War between the US and the Soviet Union that followed World War II. During the Cold War, the US Department of Defense (DOD) funded scientists to invent computer-controlled tools to be used in warplanes. Then, in the 1960s and 1970s during the Cold War, the DOD funded research into connecting military and government research computers by a decentralized network.[8] The reason was that a web-like decentralized network would greatly reduce the risk of bombs destroying vital governmental and military information. Later, these military backed scientific advances trickled down to benefit civilians in the form of the internet, and the World Wide Web.

War does not explain why people assume that since the universe is understandable then we will know its laws and be able to manipulate these laws if we invest time into carefully studying them. What is the reason for explaining this belief based on the first principle that the world is understandable? This presupposes that there is an intelligent de-

---

[7] Mills and Mills "The Invention of the War Machine," *The New Atlantis*, 10.

[8] Johnny Ryan, *A History of the Internet and the Digital Future* (London: Reaktion Books, 2010), 14, 26.

sign in the universe capable of being understood by our intelligence. One explanation for this presupposition undoubtedly is the Judeo-Christian belief, referred to in a previous chapter, which holds that since the world was created by God who is infinitely intelligent and we, by being made in His image and likeness, are also intelligent, we can understood the intelligence of his creation.

Catholicism by associating *Logos* (meaning word and reason in Greek) with Christ, through whom the Father in the love of the Holy Spirit created the world, clearly affirms that the language of the Christ as The Word is not simply mathematical but also moral.[9] In Christ, therefore, objective truth, including moral truth, is deeply personal and, in this personal sense, subjective because all "objective" truth is located in the subject, i.e. person of Christ. Many practitioners of modern science, though, only identify the truth with what they can measure. Everything else, including morality or experiences of beauty and love, are merely subjective and not essentially true since they cannot be quantified and analyzed according to the modern scientific method.[10] The famous German theoretical physicist Werner Heisenberg, active during World War II, is an example of a foremost scientist who only identifies truth, which he calls the

---

[9] Joseph Cardinal Ratzinger, *On Conscience* (San Francisco: Ignatius Press, 2007), 67.

[10] Ratzinger, *On Conscience*, 50.

"objective aspect of reality," with what modern science can measure.

Heisenberg stated in 1927, "Natural science is to some extent the way we approach the objective aspect of reality…Religious faith, on the contrary, is the expression of a subjective decision, by means of which we determine for ourselves the values by which we direct ourselves in life."[11] Heisenberg further believed that as people realize that the only truth in the world is that which can be measured by the modern scientific method, "traditional morality will also very rapidly break down, and things will happen that are more frightful than anything we can yet imagine."[12] As World War II progressed, his fears proved right. Ratzinger agrees with Heisenberg that the loss of morality is due to relegating morality to the realm of subjective feelings while recognizing truth as only discoverable by scientists. He warns, "Science becomes pathological and a threat to life when it takes leave of the moral order of human life, becomes autonomous, and no longer recognizes any standard but its own capabilities."[13]

Since modern science is defined by the scientific meth-

---

[11] Joseph Cardinal Ratzinger, *Truth and Tolerance: Christian Belief and World Religions*, trans. Henry Taylor (San Francisco: Ignatius Press, 2004), 138-139.

[12] Ratzinger, *Truth and Tolerance*, 139.

[13] Ratzinger, *Truth and Tolerance*, 158.

od of hypothesizing followed by empirically verifying or denying the hypothesis, it cannot as a method bear within itself an objective moral code. For example, an atheist and a believer can both, without contradicting their beliefs, follow the same method to successfully build a car. The philosophical, moral world view of the atheist and believer comes prior to following the method and is not contained in the car building instructions.

Morality is found in philosophies and religions that are open to truth that cannot be precisely measured, such as justice, goodness and evil. These moral truths, not attainable by the scientific method that is limited to measuring quantities, are the standard that determines whether scientific inventions are being used in good or bad ways. Without such a moral standard, there exists no measure by which to determine whether or not to drop atomic bombs on an innocent population, such as occurred during World War II, an action condemned by Pope St. John Paul II, or to systematically eliminate certain human ethnicities and cultures from the earth.

In our great modern fascination and appreciation of science may we take heed of another great pope's words, Benedict XVI's, who in his encyclical *Spe Salvi* reminds us that, "It is not science that redeems man: man is redeemed by love."¹⁴ This love that the Holy Father is referring to is love formed by moral and doctrinal truths provided by faith, some of which are accessible to human reason when it is open to discovering truth as a moral quality within the rationality of the universe.

**Significant Sub-Atomic Scientists**

*Marie Curie (1867-1934)*

Curie was a Polish physicist and chemist. She coined the term radioactivity and used this term in reference to instability in certain atoms, in particular uranium. This explanation led later scientists to discover that atoms are made up by even smaller particles. Curie tragically died from aplastic anemia caused by radiation exposure.¹⁵

*Ernest Rutherford (1871-1937)*

Ernest Rutherford was a New Zealand physicist and chemist who is considered the father of nuclear physics. He

---

¹⁴ Benedict XVI, "Spe Salvi," The Vatican, http://w2.vatican.va/content/benedict-xvi/en/encyclicals/documents/hf_ben-xvi_enc_20071130_spe-salvi.html, no. 26.

¹⁵ Naomi Pasachoff, *Marie Curie: The Science of Radioactivity* (Oxford: Oxford University Press, 1996), 36-38, 99, 102, 105.

studied radioactive decay and is credited with being the first to split the atom in 1917. Upon so doing, he discovered a sub-atomic particle, the positively charged proton.[16]

*Niels Bohr (1885-1962)*

Niels Bohr was a Danish physicist who came up with a model of the atom called the Bohr model. According to the Bohr model, an atom has a nucleus at its center around which orbit electrons. Bohr also discovered that when electrons drop from one level of energy to another, determined by their orbit, they release energy.[17] Bohr's work was a further development of an earlier English chemist and physicist John Dalton (1766-1844). Dalton theorized that matter is made up of little particles he called atoms that can be combined into various compounds, such as water comprised of oxygen and hydrogen.[18]

---

[16] J. L. Heilbron, *Ernest Rutherford and the Explosion of Atoms* (Oxford: Oxford University Press, 2003), 54, 97, 111-115.

[17] Helge Kragh, *Niels Bohr and the Quantum Atom: The Bohr Model of Atomic Structure 1913-1925* (Oxford: Oxford University Press, 2012), 16, 64-65.

[18] John Dalton, *A New System of Chemical Philosophy*, Part I (London: S. Russell, 1808), 275-276.

**Bohr's Model**

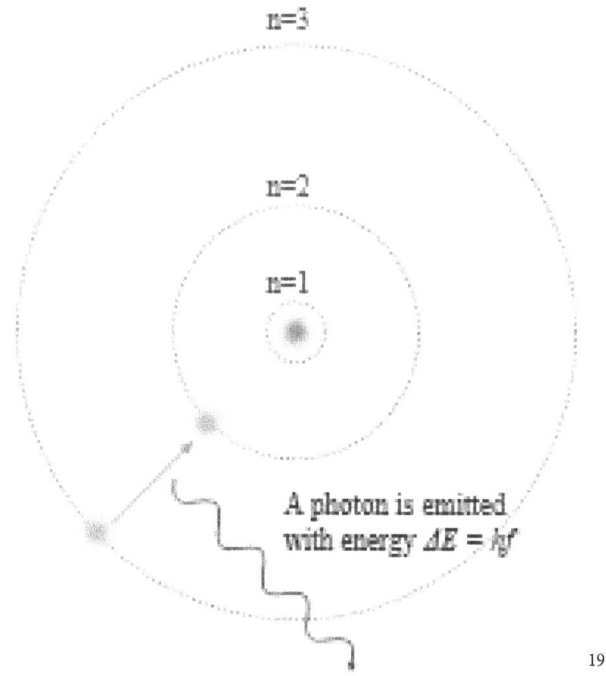

*Enrico Fermi (1901-1954)*

Enrico Fermi was an Italian physicist who in 1938, shortly before World War II, proposed the possibility of splitting apart particles of an uranium atom's nuclei into atomic fragments. This breaking apart is called fission.[20] The opposite effect is fusion, which occurs when atomic

---

[19] User:Cepheus, "Bohr model," diagram, http://commons.wikimedia.org/wiki/File%3ABohr_model.svg.

[20] Emilio Segre, *Enrico Fermi, Physicist* (Chicago: University of Chicago Press, 1970), 110-112.

particles are fused together. In both cases, the result is the production of energy in vast quantities. The atomic bombs dropped over Hiroshima and Nagasaki were fission bombs.

*Werner Heisenberg (1901-1976)*

Heisenberg (1901-1976) was a German theoretical physicist who is famous for his Uncertainty Principle. According to this principle, it is impossible to precisely know at the same time the speed and location of the tiny, subatomic particle called the electron because the scientific observer's use of light, which bounces off the electron, will necessarily influence either the electron's position or its velocity.[21]

---

[21] Speed and location are examples of properties that physicists call non-commuting observables. As explained by Steven Gimbel, "When we measure the value of one of these non-commuting observables precisely, the other one no longer has a value at all. When we measure the position of an object, it ceased to have a speed. Instead it's in a state of what physicists call superposition, that is, it simultaneously has and not has every possible speed it could have." Steven Gimbel, *An Introduction to Formal Logic* (Chantilly: The Teaching Company, 2016), 532; Werner Heisenberg, *Physics and Philosophy: The Revolution in Modern Science* (New York: HarperCollins Publishers, 2007), x.

**Quantum Theorists**

Quantum theory, whose beginning theorist is considered to be the German theoretical physicist Max Planck (1858-1947), developed out of the research done on subatomic particles and on electromagnetic fields. Since we have already roughly covered the history of the modern subatomic particles, I will briefly introduce you to a few scientists who studied such fields. The English scientist Michael Faraday (1791-1867) and his friend the Scotsman James Clerk Maxwell (1831-1879) proposed the concept of an electromagnetic field in which magnetism, electricity, and light are interrelated.[22] Quantum theory studies both wave-like structures, present in electromagnetic fields, and subatomic particles. According to this theory, on the subatomic level the universe appears to be undetermined and not deterministic. This explains why some changes on the subatomic level can only be determined by guess work based on probability since the change only occurs with a limited amount (*quantum* in Latin) of subatomic particles and not in a universal manner. This means that the universe when studied on the level of its smallest particles and waves is fundamentally undetermined, based on probability, and not

---

[22] Nancy Forbes, and Basil Mahon Faraday, Maxwell and the Electromagnetic Field (New York: Prometheus Books, 2014), 11-13, 17-18.

determined as Isaac Newton held.²³

**Biological Scientific Discoveries**

*Thomas H. Morgan (1866-1945)*

Thomas H. Morgan was an American evolutionary biologist and geneticist who discovered that genes carried on chromosomes contain instructions for how living organisms are to develop. His research was based on the Austrian Augustinian friar Gregor Mendel's (1822-1884) research on traits in pea plants. Mendel discovered that certain traits of pea plants are passed down to subsequent pea plants. Morgan further specified how this happens.²⁴

*Francis Crick (1916-2004)*

Francis Crick was an English molecular biologist who, along with the American James Watson, in 1953 studied the

---

²³ Christopher T. Baglow, *Faith, Science & Reason: Theology on the Cutting Edge* (Woodridge: Midwest Theological Forum, 2009), 233.

²⁴ Ian Shine, Sylvia Wrobel, *Thomas Hunt Morgan: Pioneer of Genetics* (Lexington: University Press of Kentucky, 1976), x, 46-50; Thomas Hunt Morgan, "A Critique of the Theory of Evolution," 93, Project Gutenberg, http://www.gutenberg.org/files/30701/30701-h/30701-h.htm#page91.

DNA molecule (Deoxyribonucleic acid), the matter out of which genes are made of. In studying DNA, he learned how traits are passed from an older cell to a newly generated cell. According to Crick and Watson, DNA is structured in such a way that allows it to easily transmit its genetic code. The structure of DNA consists of two twisted connected strands, the double helix, that spiral around each other. These two strands transmit their genetic code to new cells.[25]

Double Helix

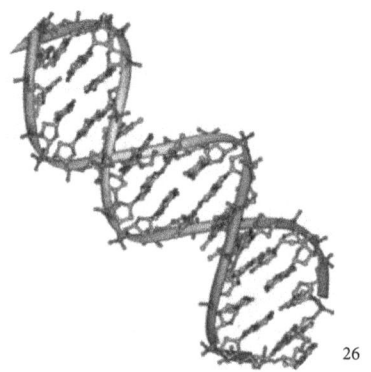

[26]

---

[25] Mat Ridley, *Francis Crick: Discover of the Genetic Code* (New York: Harper Collins, 2006), 2, 41-51, 70.

[26] Jerome Walker, Dennis Myts, "DNA double helix," diagram, http://commons.wikimedia.org/wiki/File%3ADNA_ double_helix_45.PNG.

*Francis Collins (1950- )*

Francis Collins is an American physician and geneticist who led the Human Genome Project that worked on mapping out the human genome. He once held that religion was contrary to science and identified himself as an atheist. Eventually, he converted to Christianity and published in 2007 his book *The Language of God* where he describes the genetic code as "our own instruction book previously known only to God."[27]

**Modern Physics**

*Albert Einstein (1879-1955)*

Einstein was a German born, US citizen who rejected Isaac Newton's belief that matter and space are absolute realities that can be measured exactly with reference to an immovable substance called ether. According to Einstein, ether does not exist, and space and time are not absolute realities but rather relative realities that, when influenced by gravity and acceleration, expand and contract, in the

---

[27] Francis S. Collins, *The Language of God* (New York: Simon & Schuster, 2006), 3.

case of space, and dilate and narrow, in the case of time.[28]

*George Lemaitre (1894-1966)*

Lemaitre was a Belgian priest and physicist who helped Einstein to arrive at his relativity theories. One obstacle that prevented Einstein from developing his relativity theories was that he believed the universe had existed for an infinite amount of time and is neither expanding nor contracting. Lemaitre, with his theory of the "primeval atom" later called the Big Bang, convinced Einstein, during a lecture Lemaitre gave in 1933, that the universe was once contained in an extremely, dense point of matter that exploded outward causing our universe to be ever expanding.[29]

**Quiz 9 for Chapter 9**

1-4. According to the historian A.J. Taylor, "War has always been the mother of invention." In a paragraph, explain why war motivates people to innovate. Include specific scientific innovations from World War I and from the Cold War. (Write a minimum of four sentences.)

---

[28] Baglow, *Faith, Science & Reason*, 142-144; Walter Isaacson, *Einstein: His Life and Universe* (New York: Simon & Schuster, 2007), 107-140, 189-225.

[29] Baglow, *Faith, Science & Reason*, 143.

Chapter 9 Radical Scientific Discoveries    247

5-8. With reference to the Judeo-Christian belief in creation, explain why war only provides the occasion for invention but does not provide the reason why man has the capacity to innovate. Also, explain how in Catholicism truth is not simply identified with scientific discovery. (Write a minimum of four sentences.)

9. Chose a sub-atomic scientist from the following list and describe his or her scientific discoveries: Marie Curie, Ernest Rutherford, Niels Bohr, Enrico Fermi, and Werner Heisenberg. In answering, you may include a simple diagram.

10. Choose a quantum theorist from the following list and describe his scientific discoveries: Max Planck, James Clerk Maxwell, and Michael Faraday.

11. Choose a biologist from the following list and describe his scientific discoveries: Thomas H. Morgan, Francis Crick, and Francis Collins.

12. Choose a physicist from the following list and describe his scientific discoveries: Albert Einstein and Fr. George Lemaitre.

# Chapter 10

## The Cold War: Capitalism and Communism

**Introduction**

On August 23rd, 1939, the Soviet Union signed a non-aggression pact called the Molotov-Ribbentrop pact with Nazi Germany. This was signed eight days before Germany invaded Poland, which resulted in World War II. Part of the pact included a relatively secret agreement between Germany and the Soviet Union in how to divide between themselves Northeastern, Southeastern, and Eastern Europe. This agreement was not officially admitted by the Soviet Union until 1987 when Gorbachev referred to the Molotov-Ribbentrop pact during a speech critical of Stalin's leadership. In 1989, Soviet leaders in Moscow confirmed that the Molotov-Ribbentrop Pact included a deal by which Germany and the Soviet Union divided up Eastern Europe between themselves. These public revelations contributed to the desire shared by Eastern European countries to be free from Soviet rule.[1] Finally, in 1991 the Soviet Union of-

---

[1] Some of these so-called Eastern European countries, such as Poland, are more properly categorized as Central European

ficially ceased to exist, and many countries gained their freedom back.

The brief history above is little known, especially since during the latter part of World War II the Soviet Union fought on the side of the Allies. It did so after Germany broke its non-aggression pact by invading the Soviet Union in 1941. The following year, on January 1st, 1942, the Soviet Union became a member of the Allies by signing the Declaration of the United Nations. The signers on the document included, "the United States, the United Kingdom, the Union of Soviet Socialist Republics, China, Australia, Belgium, Canada, Costa Rica, Cuba, Czechoslovakia, Dominican Republic, El Salvador, Greece, Guatemala, Haiti, Honduras, India, Luxembourg, Netherlands, New Zealand, Nicaragua, Norway, Panama, Poland, South Africa, and Yugoslavia."[2] Its aim was to defeat the Nazi-led Axis powers. The Declaration clearly states:

> Being convinced that complete victory over their enemies is essential to defend life, liberty, independence and religious freedom,

---

countries. George J. Neimanis, *The Collapse of the Soviet Empire: A View from Riga* (Westport: Praeger Publishers, 1997), 53-54.

[2] "Declaration by the United Nations, January 1, 1942," Yale Law School, Lillian Goldman Library, The Avalon Project, http://avalon.law.yale.edu/20th_century/decade03.asp.

and to preserve human rights and justice in their own lands as well as in other lands, and that they are now engaged in a common struggle against savage and brutal forces seeking to subjugate the world,

DECLARE:

(1) Each Government pledges itself to employ its full resources, military or economic, against those members of the Tripartite Pact: and its adherents with which such government is at war.

(2) Each Government pledges itself to cooperate with the Governments signatory hereto and not to make a separate armistice or peace with the enemies.

The foregoing declaration may be adhered to by other nations which are, or which may be, rendering material assistance and contributions in the struggle for victory over Hitlerism.[3]

---

[3] "Declaration by the United Nations, January 1, 1942," Yale Law School.

After World War II ended, the true colors of the Soviet Union were revealed as it gained control of the countries it was to rule according to the 1939 Molotov-Ribbentrop pact with Nazi Germany. Realizing this, in 1946 the Prime Minister of England, Winston Churchill, angrily denounced the USSR:

> From Stettin in the Baltic to Trieste in the Adriatic an 'Iron Curtain' has descended across the continent. Behind that line lie all the capitals of the ancient states of Central and Eastern Europe. Warsaw, Berlin, Prague, Vienna, Budapest, Belgrade, Bucharest and Sofia; all these famous cities and the populations around them lie in what I must call the Soviet sphere, and all are subject, in one form or another, not only to Soviet influence but to a very high and in some cases increasing measure of control from Moscow.[4]

Churchill's speech signaled the beginning of the Cold

---

[4] This speech was called the "Sinews of Peace Address" given on March 5, 1946 at Westminster College. Robert Rhodes James, *Winston S. Churchill: His Complete Speeches 1897-1963 Volume VII* (Chelsea House Publishers: New York, 1983), 7285-7293.

War that lasted until 1991 when the Soviet Union was dissolved. It is called a Cold War to signify that the tension between the Soviet Union and the Western World, led by the USA, was hidden and not in the open. When wars were fought, caused by this hidden tension, it was by proxy. For example, the Vietnam War can be understood as a proxy war between the Soviet Union and the United States. The proxy for the Soviets were the North Vietnamese who were financially supported by the Soviets, and the proxy for the United States were the South Vietnamese who received both financial and military support from the US.

In this chapter, we will focus our attention on the Cold War by beginning first with Soviet Marxist ideology. Then, we will examine a number of events where tension peaked, including the Soviet Blockade in Berlin, the Korean War, the Suez Crisis, the Yom Kippur War, the Berlin Crisis, the Cuban missile crisis, the Vietnam War, the Soviet war in Afghanistan, the downing of a Korean Airplane by the Soviets, and the Able Archer 83 military exercise program. This will be followed by a concluding section on the dissolution of the Soviet Empire in 1991.

**Marxism as a Response to Capitalism**

Since historically Marxism was a response to capitalism, we will first examine how capitalism developed and took hold in much of the Western world before examining how Marxist communism took root in the east. The term capitalism originates from the Latin word *caput,* which means head, especially head of cattle. In ancient Rome, the first capitalist was, explains Florian Werner in his book *Cow: A Bovine Biography,* "someone who could call many heads his own – who, in other words, owned a large number of cows."[5] In explaining communism and other ideologies in relationship to cows, the comedian Pat Paulsen during his campaign in 1968 for the US presidency quipped:

> *You Have Two Cows*
>
> ...
>
> COMMUNISM You have two cows; the government takes both and gives you some milk.
>
> FASCISM: You have two cows; the government takes both and sells you the milk.
>
> NAZISM: You have two cows; the government takes both and shoots you.
>
> ...
>
> CAPITALISM: You have two cows; you sell one and buy a bull.[6]

---

[5] Florian Werner, *Cow: A Bovine Biography* (Quebec: Greystone Books, 2011), 15.

[6] Werner, *Cow: A Bovine Biography,* 12-13. Pat Paulsen was a comedian who ran for presidency in 1968. The quotes are from

Why is capitalistic ideology linked to cows? This is because the owner can move the heads of cattle at will. The key component of capitalism, consequently, is easy to move property that can take the form of cattle, or in more modern times, financial investments that are digitally transferred in a millisecond. Another essential component of capitalism involves self-interested businesses that own movable property for the purpose of making profit. A key element that allows businesses to flourish in a competitive environment is that the state does not set prices but rather allows the price to be determined in the market place as businesses compete for customers. According to the Scotsman Adam Smith (1723-1790) in his book *The Wealth of Nations*, written at the time capitalism was becoming a major ideology during the industrial revolution, political rulers should leave the economic market place alone since it is ruled by a self-regulating mechanism called the "invisible hand."[7]

During the industrial revolution, some people became convinced that such an invisible hand, which Adam Smith

---

his campaign. Missing from the excerpt is, "SOCIALISM: You have two cows; you give one to your neighbor... NEW DEALISM: You have two cows; the government takes both, shoots one, milks the other and throws part of the milk down the sink."

[7] Adam Smith, *The Wealth of Nations*, Gutenberg Consortia Center, "The Wealth of Nations" http://ebooks.gutenberg.us/Renascence_Editions/wealth/wealth4.html book 4, chapter 2.

only refers to once in his writings,[8] either does not exist or, if it does, is highly ineffective. Consequently, an ideology in reaction to capitalism developed called socialism that, as its name indicates, believes that man is more social by nature than competitive. The earliest socialists came from France and England. The most famous of socialists, and not one of the earliest, was Karl Marx (1818-1883). Karl Marx, along with Friedrich Engels (1820-1895), disparagingly called the socialists who preceded them utopian socialists. Supposedly, the earliest socialists were utopian since they had pious dreams of an ideal society but did not know how to actualize their dreams. In contrast, claimed Marx, in his scientific socialism, the dream of the early socialist could finally be implemented in a systematic, practical manner. His version of socialism is scientific since, Marx argued, he had discovered inevitable trends of history that once known can be sped up to its final destination point of communism, a kind of heaven on earth where the state will wither away and the distinction of classes will cease to exist.

The trends of history, explained Marx, in accordance

---

[8] Jonathan Steinberg points out, "Smith uses the idea of the invisible hand as the organizing idea and justification for free markets only once, in Book IV on foreign trade. The idea that markets are 'providential' arrangement is a later invention." Jonathan Steinberg, *European History and European Lives: 1715 to 1914*, CDs and Course Guidebook (Chantilly: Great Courses, 2003), 87.

with his materialistic version of Hegelian thought, are shaped in a dialectical manner characterized by a thesis, antithesis, and synthesis. The ultimate synthesis of history, where history as dialectics ends, is communism. Prior to communism, a political and economic system brings forth its antithesis which is resolved in a synthesis that bears within it its own dialectical tension. For example, capitalism contains within itself the seeds of socialism that is at tension with capitalism. The tension between capitalism, as the thesis, and socialism, as the antithesis, is resolved in the synthesis of communism. The driving force, or engine of the dialectical tension, are new modes of production. A new mode of production, such as the invention of the steam engine or the creation of the internet, triggers the dialectical tension which is manifested in class conflict. Only at the end of history, claimed Marx, will these tensions be resolved in a classless, communist society. To cut down the time it takes to reach the perfect synthesis of communism, people who know the trends of history can direct the forces of history by working violently or non-violently to hasten the end of communism. In describing the earthly paradise of communism, which by the way there is absolutely no scientific proof that it awaits us, Marx wrote:

1. Abolition of property in land and application of all rents of land to public purposes.

2. A heavy progressive or graduated income tax.
3. Abolition of all right of inheritance.
4. Confiscation of the property of all emigrants and rebels.
5. Centralization of credit in the hands of the State, by means of a national bank with State capital and an exclusive monopoly.
6. Centralization of the means of communication and transport in the hands of the State.
7. Extension of factories and instruments of production owned by the State; the bringing into cultivation of waste-lands, and the improvement of the soil generally in accordance with a common plan.
8. Equal liability of all to labor. Establishment of industrial armies, especially for agriculture.
9. Combination of agriculture with manufacturing industries; gradual abolition of the distinction between town and country, by a more equable distribution of the population over the country.
10. Free education for all children in public schools. Abolition of children's factory

labor in its present form. Combination of education with industrial production, &c., &c.⁹

Inspired by Marx's description of the earthly paradise that supposedly would come and by Marx's belief that once the trends of history are known the time it takes to reach this end can be shortened, in 1917 Vladimir Lenin and his Bolsheviks plunged Russia into a civil war (1917-1922), which ended with the Communist Bolsheviks emerging victorious. In 1922, Lenin officially established the Soviet Union. As described by Robert Service in *Lenin: A Biography*, Lenin was convinced that the violent upheavals he was causing were justified since, "Through Marx and Engels he [Lenin] 'knew' that the future would bring about a final and wonderful stage in world history. His life had purpose. Lenin clung to a rock of attitudes and assumptions, and on it he was able to construct almost any notions about politics and economics he wanted."[10] How could Lenin know the future? Can the scientific method, as applied to politics, give us certain scientific knowledge about the future? If it is

---

[9] Karl Marx, *The Communist Manifesto*, Project Gutenberg, "The Communist Manifesto," http://www.gutenberg.org/files/61/61.txt part II.

[10] Robert Service, *Lenin: A Biography* (London: Macmillan, 1997), 237.

claimed that science can predict the future with certainty, then does this mean that history is determined? If so, then how is it possible for anyone to hasten history to its end since the ability to choose to hasten something to its end implies the presence of free will. Free will, however, is not determined.

After Lenin died in 1924, Joseph Stalin led the Soviet Union with even greater violence, justified by the end he was supposedly hastening with his free will that, ultimately according to Marxist determinism, does not exist. This fundamental contradiction was a root cause of the collapse of the Soviet Union in 1991. During the time the Soviet Union existed in its self-contradictory state, there were spikes of tension partly caused by its own inherent illogic. We will now briefly touch upon a few of the major ones during the Cold War era.

**The Peaks of Cold War Tension**

*Soviet Blockade in Berlin*

At the end of World War II, Germany was divided into four zones: a US zone, a British zone, a French zone, and a Soviet zone. The capital of Germany, Berlin, located within the Soviet zone, was similarly divided into four sections. Three of Berlin's four sections were ruled by the western powers of the US, Britain, and France. The remaining section, located in the Eastern portion of Berlin, was ruled by the Soviet Union. With the hope of ending western rule in the three western controlled sections of Berlin, in 1948 the Soviet Union prevented the US and its allies from delivering goods (food, fuel, medical supplies etc.) to the approximately two million Germans living in the Western controlled section of Berlin. Railways, highways, and canals by which fuel, food, and other vital supplies arrived in West Berlin were all blocked by the Soviets. The Soviets also ended much of the electrical power that West Berlin relied upon.

The US and Britain responded by flying airplanes to daily deliver supplies to these Germans. The Soviets responded with low levels of harassments such as flying fighter jets close to cargo planes and by shining bright lights into the western airplanes' cockpits. During the blockade, it seemed possible that a third world war of western powers against the Soviet Union could develop. Some officials in the western countries even entertained the idea of sending in tanks into the Soviet zone of Germany in order to force the Soviets to open up the highways, canals, and railways. Fortunately, on May 12, 1949, the Soviet Union ended the harassment and lifted its blockade.[11]

---

[11] Michael Burgan, *The Berlin Airlift: Breaking the Soviet Blockade* (Minneapolis: Compass Print Books, 2008), 8-10; Hen-

*1947 Occupation Zones in Germany. Berlin is represented by the small, multicolor symbol in the red zone of the Soviets.*

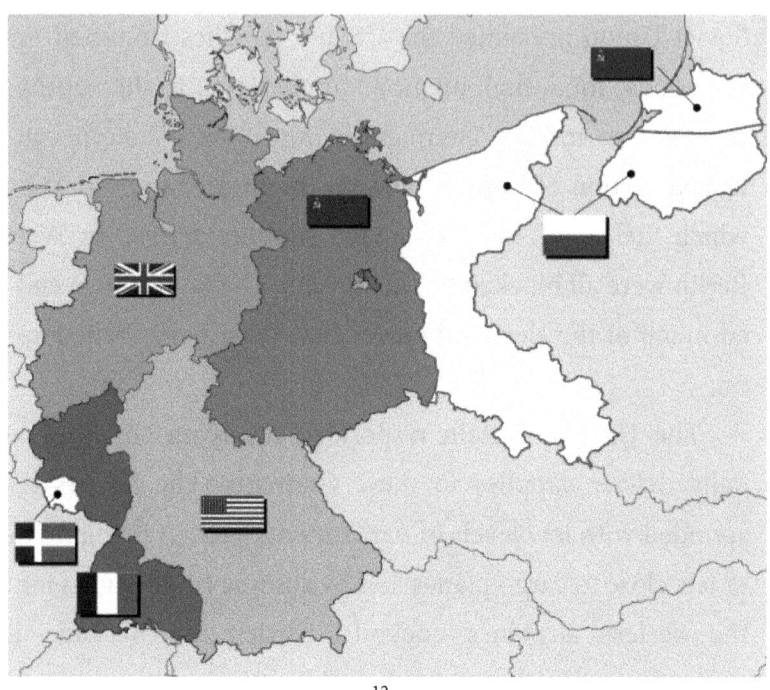

ry Ashby Turner, *The Two Germanies Since 1945* (New Haven: Yale University Press, 1987), 24-27.

[12] 52 Pickup, "Map-Germany-1947," map, http://commons.wikimedia.org/wiki/File%3AMap-Germany-1947.svg . "Occupation zone borders in Germany, 1947. The territories east of the Oder-Neisse line, under Polish and Soviet administration/annexation, are shown as white as is the likewise detached Saar protectorate. Berlin is the multinational area within the Soviet zone."

Chapter 10 The Cold War: Capitalism and Communism    263

*The Korean War*

From August 22nd, 1910, when the Korean Emperor surrendered his rule to Japan, to the remaining days of World War II, Japan governed Korea. In August of 1945, near the end of World War II, the Soviet Union entered into a war with Japan and gained control of the northern section of Korea up to the 38th parallel, which divides Korea in half. Meanwhile, the US was occupying southern Korea. The government that formed in the north was modeled on the Soviet system of governance while the southern government was modeled on the US system of governance. Tension between these two Koreas, each claiming to be the only legitimate Korea, erupted into a war on June 25th, 1950, when Soviet and Chinese backed North Korean troops invaded South Korea. With the backing of the United Nations Security Council, the US led and launched a counter-attack. On July 27th, 1953, an armistice was signed according to which Korea was divided into a Northern, communist controlled nation and a Southern, democratic nation.[13] The casualties of the UN troops, predominantly US, were 142,000, and the casualties of the Koreans was, at minimum, a million.[14] The war officially ended with the

---

[13] Max Hastings, *The Korean War* (New York: Simon & Schuster Inc., 1987), 11, 15, 25, 27, 45-54, 230-234.

[14] Hastings, *The Korean War*, 9.

signing in the demilitarized zone between North and South Korea of the "Panmunjom Declaration for Peace, Prosperity and Unification on the Korean Peninsula" by South Korean President Moon Jae-in and his North Korean counterpart Kim Jong Un on April 27, 2018.[15]

See below for a photograph taken at night of the Korean peninsula. Notice the significantly fewer lights in North Korea, indicating economic activity, compared with the lights present in South Korea.

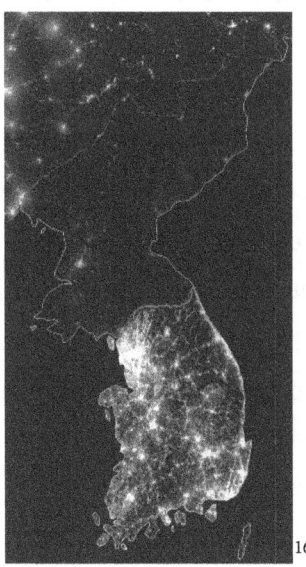

[15] Eli Meixler, "Here's What Kim Jong Un and Moon Jae-In Said to Each Other in Their Historic First Meeting" (April 27, 2018), Online at https://time.com/5257125/kim-jong-un-moon-jae-in-meeting-transcript/

[16] NASA, "KoreaAtNight20121205 NASA.png," photograph, http://commons.wikimedia.org/wiki/File%3AKoreaAtNight2012

*Suez Crisis and the Yom Kippur War*

On May 14th, 1948, the same day that the British mandate of Palestine officially ended, the State of Israel declared its existence. That day, in establishing the Jewish state, David Ben-Gurion read from the Scroll of Independence:

> ...by virtue of our national and intrinsic right and on the strength of the resolution of the United Nations General Assembly we hereby declare the establishment of a Jewish state in Palestine, which shall be known as the State of Israel.[17]

---

1205_NASA.png. "An image showing the Korean peninsula at night in the year 2012. A composite image, constructed using cloud-free night images taken by the National Aeronautics and Space Administration (NASA) and the National Oceanic and Atmospheric Administration (NOAA) Suomi National Polar-orbiting Partnership (NPP) satellite. These photographs were taken with the Visible Infrared Imaging Radiometer Suite (VIIRS), and the composite was published by NASA on December 5, 2012. I modified the image by removing the lights from ships on the open ocean to highlight the contrast between North Korea and South Korea."

[17] H. H. Ben Sasson, *A History of the Jewish People* (Cambridge: Harvard University Press, 1976), 1058.

The very next day, armies from the surrounding Arab nations invaded Israel in a coordinated attack. The invading nations included Egypt, Syria, Jordan, and Iraq. The Arab-Israeli war ended in the beginning of 1949 as armistices between Israel and its Arab neighbors were signed under the supervision of the UN negotiator and US citizen, Ralph Bunche. For his peace keeping efforts, Bunche was awarded a Nobel Prize in 1950.[18] During the conflict, the United States attempted to play a neutral role in order not to allow Middle East unrest to disrupt the balance of power of the Cold War that could lead to a third World War.[19]

This balance of power between the USSR and the USA came close to being gravely disturbed when Israel, backed by the Western powers of Britain and France, invaded Egypt in 1956 in order gain control of the Suez canal. Believing that it was in their mutual interest, the United States and the Soviet Union both wisely insisted that Israel withdraw its forces from Egypt. Israel complied.[20]

During the 1973 Arab-Israeli War, the Soviet Union and the United did not collaborate together in order to

---

[18] "Ralph Bunche – Facts," Nobelprize.org. Nobel Media AB http://www.nobelprize.org/nobel_prizes/peace/laureates/1950/bunche-facts.html.

[19] "The Arab-Israeli War of 1948," U.S. Department of the State: Office of the Historian, http://history.state.gov/milestones/1945-1952/arab-israeli-war.

[20] Ben Sasson, *A History of the Jewish People*, 1080-1081.

avoid Cold War tensions from escalating. In this war, the Soviets sided with the Arab nations by supplying them with arms while the United States allied itself with Israel. The war was initiated by a coalition of Arab states, headed by Egypt and Syria, and began on the holiest day of the Jewish year, Yom Kippur, also known as the Day of Atonement. Fortunately, this war lasted less than a month when on October 25th the United Nations convinced the two sides to end it.[21]

The box below indicates the important water passage way of the Suez Canal. The Suez Canal connects the Mediterranean Sea and the Indian Ocean by way of the Red Sea.

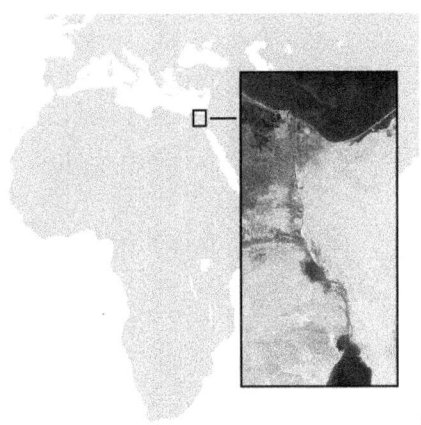

22

---

[21] Abraham Rabinovich, *The Yom Kippur War: The Epic Encounter That Transformed the Middle East* (New York: Schocken Books), 3, 13-14, 30, 54, 86, 324, 432, 476.

[22] "Canal de Suez.jpg," map and photograph, http://commons.wikimedia.org/wiki/File:Canal_de_Suez.jpg.

*Berlin Crisis*

On June 4th of 1961, the Soviet Union threatened the Cold War bipolar, balance of power by requiring in an ultimatum that western nations remove their military forces from West Berlin. The West was given six months to comply. The US, Britain, and France, though, refused to comply. After three years of intense negotiations, the Soviets in 1961 responded by building a well-guarded wall to separate East Berlin from West Berlin. Below is a diagram of the wall.[23]

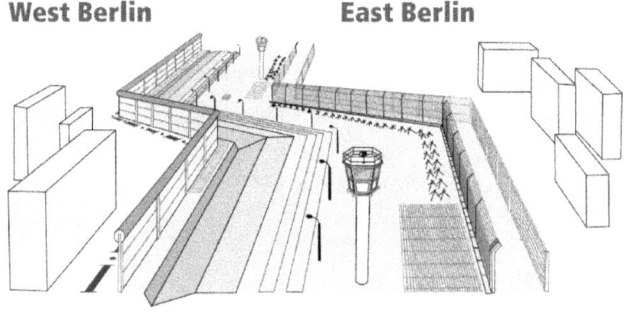

---

"The location of the Suez Canal, which connects the Mediterranean and the Indian Ocean via the Red Sea."

[23] "The Berlin Crisis, 1958–1961," U.S. Department of the State: Office of the Historian, http://history.state.gov/milestones/1953-1960/berlin-crises.

[24] Ericmetro, "Structure of Berlin Wall," http://commons.wikimedia.org/wiki/File%3AStructure_of_Berlin_Wall.svg.

*Cuban Missile Crisis*

In 1902, the former Spanish Colony of Cuba gained its independence from US occupation. From 1902 to 1958, Cuba was ruled by pro-US leaders. The final pro-US leader was General Fulgencio Batista. Batista served as Cuba's president from 1940-1944 and from 1952-1958. In 1958, Fidel Castro, who favored the Soviet Union, successfully overthrew the Batista regime. The United States CIA reacted by secretly planning to overthrow Fidel Castro in April of 1961. This failed invasion of Cuba is called the Bay of Pigs.[25]

In October of 1962, Cuba once again became the epicenter of tension between the United States and the Soviet Union. The tension appeared to come close to the brink of nuclear war. Prior to 1962, the Soviet Union had secretly built silos on Cuba from which to house and launch missiles and had sent 42,000 armed Soviet soldiers to the island. Since the Caribbean Island country of Cuba is a little under one hundred miles from the US coast, this posed a grave threat to US security. When the US Air Force conclusively confirmed that these missile facilities had been built in Cuba in order to receive the Soviet's missiles, Cold War tensions escalated dramatically. To prevent the missiles

---

[25] Priscilla Roberts, *Cuban Missile Crisis: The Essential Reference Guide* (Santa Barbara: ABC-CLIO, 2012), xi-xiv.

270　　Western Civilization: Renaissance to Modern Times

from being delivered by the Soviets, the US Navy blockaded Cuba's ports. The US also insisted that missiles already in Cuba be returned to the Soviet Union and asserted the US will prevent any further missiles from being delivered to Cuba. Finally, on November 21$^{st}$, 1962, the US President John F. Kennedy ended the blockade around Cuba after the Soviet Union agreed to reclaim their missiles deployed on Cuba. President Kennedy also promised the Soviet Premier Nikita Khrushchev that the US would never again secretly invade Cuba.[26]

Notice how close the Southern tip of Florida is from Cuba, less than one hundred miles away.

[26] Roberts, *Cuban Missile Crisis*, xv-xix, 252.

[27] CIA, "Cuba rel94.jpg," map, http://commons.wikimedia.org/wiki/File%3ACuba_rel94.jpg.

*Vietnam War*

The Vietnam War (1955-1975) between North Vietnamese and South Vietnamese is another example of a proxy war of the Cold War era. Through the North Vietnamese, the Soviet Union fought against the US, which was supporting the South Vietnamese. The US aided the South in order to prevent communism from spreading and to contain the influence of the Soviet Union in accordance with the Truman doctrine of containment that was established partly in reaction to the Greek civil war (1946-1949) between communists and anticommunists.[28] In 1975, North Vietnam successfully defeated South Vietnam and began unifying the country under one communist government.[29] Below is one tactic of guerrilla warfare that the Northern Vietnamese used against their southern opponent that was backed by the US superpower.

---

[28] The US Marshall Plan (1948-1952) is also traceable to this time. This plan was named after the Secretary of State George Marshall. Its goal was to rebuild European countries economic infrastructure, devastated by World War II, after the efficient US business model. The US provided the funds to do so as long as certain criteria were met.

[29] Mark Atwood Lawrence, *The Vietnam War: A Concise International History* (Oxford: Oxford University Press, 2008), 1-8, 36-37, 94-95.

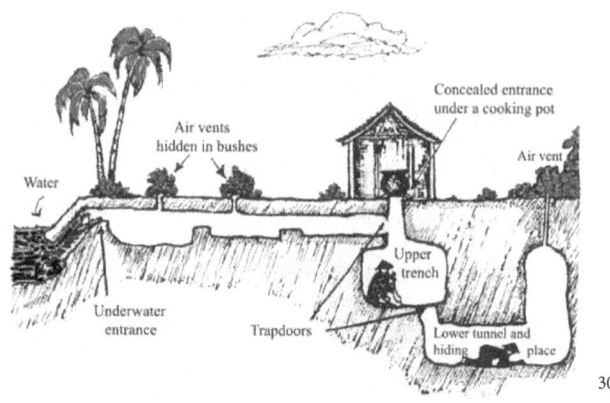

*War in Afghanistan*

The War in Afghanistan (1979 to 1989), fought by the Soviet Union against US backed Afghan forces, is similar to the US and Soviet involvement in the Vietnamese war between South Vietnam and North Vietnam. In 1979, the Soviets invaded Afghanistan to install a pro-Soviet regime. To keep Soviet influence contained, the US, under the leadership of President Ronald Reagan, armed and financially backed Afghan anti-Soviet forces called the Afghan Mujahedeen. The now infamous wealthy Saudi, and co-founder of al-Qaeda, Osama bin Laden, worked with the CIA as a

---

[30] United States Army, "Vietcong tunnels-USAR.jpg," diagram, http://commons.wikimedia.org/wiki/File%3AVietcong_tunnels-USAR.jpg . "Cross-sectional diagram of Vietcong tunnel system used by the communist insurgents during the Vietnam War."

Chapter 10 The Cold War: Capitalism and Communism    273

financier who distributed US funds to the Afghan Mujahedeen. According to the CIA officer Milt Bearden, who was stationed at the CIA presence in Islamabad, "Actually [bin Laden] did some very good things ... he put a lot of money in a lot of right places in Afghanistan."[31] In 1989, the US-backed Afghan forces successfully caused the Soviets to withdraw from Afghanistan in defeat.[32]

During the Afghan War, two incidents even further heightened Cold War friction between the US and the Soviet Union that could have sparked an all-out war. On September 1, 1983, a South Korean airplane (KE007) was flying from New York City to Seoul. Evidence indicates that a Soviet missile shot it down over the Sea of Japan. All the 269 crew members and passengers died.[33] Another incident that also occurred in 1983 is the Able Archer 83 military exercise that NATO began. The exercise was interpreted by the Soviet Union as being an actual preparation for war. The

---

[31] Panagiotis Dimitrakis, *The Secret War in Afghanistan: The Soviet Union, China and Anglo-American Intelligence in the Afghan War* (New York: I.B. Tauris Co, Ltd., 2013), 183.

[32] Panagiotis Dimitrakis, *The Secret War in Afghanistan: The Soviet Union, China and Anglo-American Intelligence in the Afghan War* (New York: I.B. Tauris Co, Ltd., 2013), x, xiii, 183-184, 231, 239.

[33] Alexander Dallin, *Black Box: KAL 007 and the Superpowers* (University of California Press: Berkeley, 1985), ix, 2-4, 47.

Soviets responded by preparing for a nuclear war.[34]

*Flight Map of Korean Airlines Flight KE 007*

## The Collapse of the Soviet Union and End of the Cold War

During the Soviet's Afghan War, the Soviet Union's economy was performing poorly. Due to the mystery of human freedom, it is not possible to clearly and distinctly determine what caused the Soviet economy to fail. There is some evidence, though, that the Soviet planned economy

---

[34] Peter Vincent Pry, *War Scare: Russia and America on the Nuclear Brink* (Westport: Praeger Publishers, 1999), 34-41.

[35] Mgarin73, "Flight Map of Korean Airlines Flight 007," map, http://commons.wikimedia.org/wiki/File%3AKAL007.svg, (accessed February 22, 2015).

was doomed to fail from the very beginning when it was established in 1922. Due to differences of particular cases, which can vary substantially from one location to another and from one time to another, it is not possible for a government to determine prices of goods that adequately balances the supply of the good with the demand of the good. Also, this centralized system of price control effectively eliminates a profit incentive of companies and employers to produce.

Another reason that explains the Soviet Union's economic collapse was its inflexible system of governance, resistance to change and reform, and the Soviet Union's high military expenses. The latter one may have been the most significant factor for the breakup of the Soviet system. This is particularly evident in the Soviet-Afghan war (1979-1989). The amount of money it cost for the Soviets to fund this failed war may have put their entire economic system in jeopardy. Not surprisingly, a few years after the war ended, the Soviet Union officially ceased to exist.[36] The end of the Soviet Union came under the leadership of the Mikhail Gorbachev. Gorbachev did not think that the highly centralized system of the Soviet Union over a vast amount of

---

[36] Panagiotis Dimitrakis, *The Secret War in Afghanistan: The Soviet Union, China and Anglo-American Intelligence in the Afghan War* (New York: I.B. Tauris Co, Ltd., 2013), x, xiii, 183-184, 231, 239.

territory could survive. In 1991, the Soviet Union was dissolved, and Boris Yeltsin was elected as the president of the New Russian Republic, bringing an end to the Cold War.

The first set of images below indicates the territory that Russia, which controlled the Soviet Union, lost when the Soviet Union collapsed in 1991. The graph indicates how, since the collapse, the Russian economy has been steadily improving.

**The Soviet Union's Territory**

*Russia's Current Territory*

[37]

---

[37] Ssolbergj, "Union of Soviet Socialist Republics (orthographic projection).svg," http://commons.wikimedia.org/wiki/File%3AUnion_of_Soviet_Socialist_Republics_(orthographic_projection).svg, (accessed February 22, 2015).

Chapter 10 The Cold War: Capitalism and Communism    277

38

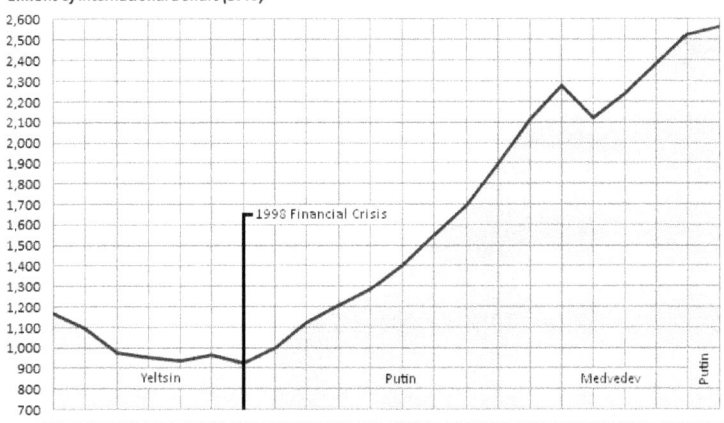

39

---

[38] FutureTrillionaire, "Russia on the globe with Crimea marked as claimed," map, http://commons.wikimedia.org/wiki/File%3ARussian_Federation_(orthographic_projection)_-_Crimea_disputed.svg.

[39] LokiiT, "Russian economy since fall of Soviet Union.PNG," graph, http://commons.wikimedia.org/wiki/File%3ARussian_economy_since_fall_of_Soviet_Union.PNG.

## Quiz 10 for Chapter 10

1-2. What were the public and secret agreements of the Molotov-Ribbentrop pact?

    1.

    2.

3-10. Contrast the Cold War with the all-out war of World War II.

| Cold War | World War II |
| --- | --- |
| 3. | 4. |
| 5. | 6. |
| 7. | 8. |
| 9. | 10. |

11-18. Compare and contrast Capitalism with Marxist Communism.

| Capitalism | Marxist Communism |
|---|---|
| 11. | 12. |
| 13. | 14. |
| 15. | 16. |
| 17. | 18. |

19-22.

Choose one of the following Cold War events and describe it in a brief paragraph of a minimum of five sentences: the Soviet Blockade in Berlin, the Korean War, the Suez Crisis, the Yom Kippur War, the Berlin Crisis, the Cuban missile crisis, the Vietnam War, the Soviet war in Afghanistan, the downing of a Korean Airplane by the Soviets, and the Able Archer 83 military exercise program.

# Chapter 11

## Post-Modern Times

**Introduction**

The chaos and irrationality of the two World Wars, the Cold wars, and all the other wars of the twentieth century led people to ask very fundamental questions in particular the same question Pontius Pilate asked Christ, "What is truth?" Is truth a stable reality that persists throughout the changes of history, even terribly violent ones, or is truth only something that is created by humans according to the time they are in and experiences they face? Is chaos and not order and reason the most fundamental reality that exists? If so, does this mean that ultimately truth is but one era's understanding of chaos and irrationality? Does our mind correspond to being, as Plato and Aristotle claimed, or rather, as Immanuel Kant asserted, since it is impossible to know being, it is likewise impossible to bring our minds into correspondence with the reality of the world? Do we know the world only by conforming our experience of reality according to the categories of our mind?[1]

A twentieth-century movement called postmodernism attempted to respond to these questions. Many of its proponents had a strong nihilistic tendency in their approach to reality. Whereas the modern enlightenment-influenced world view was to simply accept that since the world is evidentially logical, rational, and knowable, therefore we can understand the laws by which the universe operates. In contrast, many postmodernists argued that the world is not fundamentally logical, rational, and knowable, and, consequently, the only way we can know it is by creating truth that suits our historical context.

In studying the phenomena of postmodernism, we will first examine how it was understood by certain influential thinkers. Then, we will see how this thought was translated into action. Finally, we will take a brief look at how certain architecture represent postmodern thought. For the pur-

---

[1] Immanuel Kant, *Critique of Pure Reason*, trans. J.M.D. Meiklejohn (London: Bell and Daldy, 1872), xxviii. "It has hitherto been assumed that our cognition must conform to the objects…Let us then make the experiment whether we may not be more successful in metaphysics, if we assume that the objects must conform to our cognition." Up to now it has been assumed that all our cognition must conform to the objects; but … let us once try whether we do not get farther with the problems of metaphysics by assuming that the objects must conform to our cognition."

pose of this chapter, I will be focusing on a postmodern approach that Philip Cary labels as "left wing postmodernism" in contrast with right wing postmodernism. According to left wing post modernism, the modern project that began around the time of the Enlightenment views all of reality as logical and capable of being understood in a clear and distinct manner. In so exalting reason, modernists at the same time, deem traditions and traditional thought as without merit and irrational. Left wing postmodernists criticized modernists by pointing out that modern thought cannot escape from a tradition since every approach to reality necessarily includes terms that are defined within a tradition. Since tradition is irrational, argue postmodernists in accordance with modernists, this means that ultimately any claim to reason is irrational since it necessarily justifies its terms by appealing to authority within a tradition. Ultimately, this means that every tradition, including the tradition of modernity, is determined by the degree of power an individual has and not by his ability to actually reason.[2] In contrast with modernists and left wing postmodernists, right wing post modernists, as explained by Cary, maintain that tradition is not irrational but rather provides:

> the context for rationality ... Tradition is

---

[2] Philip Cary, *The History of Christian Theology*, Lectures 19-36 (Chantilly: The Teaching Company, 2008), 222-223.

where you learn to reason. Tradition is where you learn to think. Tradition is where you learn the skills of thinking and reasoning, and indeed speaking with language.... Think what happens when a two-year-old begins to learn to speak. He learns language from his mother; we speak of a mother tongue and he learns to be able to say things like "No!" Wonderful. Two-year-olds love to say no, right? Language gives them the ability to be critical. Traditions breed critical thought; traditions are the context for critical reasoning. Traditions don't have to be authoritarian and ignorant; traditions can support reason.[3]

## Post-Modern Thought

The mental shift from viewing the world as understandable in itself to viewing the world as only understandable according to the structures of our mind, or according to a democratic consensus, or even according to the mind of a dictator that is later set as the standard for truth, had a profound impact on western civilization. For this reason, in

---

[3] Cary, *The History of Christian Theology*, Lectures 19-36, 222-223.

this section we will focus our attention on understanding the postmodern movement by beginning with the French philosopher Jean-François Lyotard, who will be followed by Sigmund Freud, Michel Foucault, and Jacques Derrida.

*Jean-François Lyotard (1924-1998)*

The term postmodern was defined in 1979 by Jean-François Lyotard in his book *The Postmodern Condition.* According to Lyotard, postmodernism is anti-metanarrative. Those who understand history from the perspective of a metanarrative believe that all of history is shaped by a single logical story. In the Christian metanarrative, as stated by Revelation chapter one, verse eight, the beginning of human history begins with Christ as the alpha, first letter of the Greek Alphabet, and will be fulfilled by Christ as the omega, last letter of the Greek alphabet. The fulfillment of history will occur when Christ returns to judge the living and the dead and bring an end to time as we experience it currently. The Christian Christo-centric metanarrative, along with any other type of metanarrative, even scientific ones, Lyotard rejects as having any validity. According to him:

> Simplifying to the extreme, I define postmodern as incredulity toward metanarratives. This incredulity is undoubtedly a

product of progress in the sciences: but that progress in turn presupposes it. To the obsolescence of the metanarrative apparatus of legitimation corresponds, most notably, the crisis of metaphysical philosophy and of the university institution which in the past relied on it. The narrative function is losing its functors, its great hero, its great dangers, its great voyages, its great goal. It is being dispersed in clouds of narrative language elements—narrative, but also denotative, prescriptive, descriptive, and so on. Conveyed within each cloud are pragmatic valencies specific to its kind. Each of us lives at the intersection of many of these. However, we do not necessarily establish stable language combinations, and the properties of the ones we do establish are not necessarily communicable.[4]

By denying that metanarratives have an essential validity, Lyotard is essentially arguing that all we can do is tolerate the meaningless of life, since life has no real meaning

---

[4] Jean-François Lyotard, *The Post Modern Condition: A Report on Knowledge*, trans. Geoff Bennington and Brian Massumi (Minneapolis: University of Minnesota Press, 1984), xxiv.

behind it. Once life loses ultimate meaning, though, as the famous Viennese psychiatrist Viktor E. Frankl points out, then when the experience of life becomes burdensome it becomes exceedingly difficult to persevere in living. A why for life, argues Frankl in his work on logos therapy, enables us to survive the how of life, and, therefore, is healing.[5] Metanarratives provide an ultimate why, i.e. reason, for living. According to Christianity, because Christianity is based on the ultimate truth who is Christ, it is the most fundamentally true metanarrative.

*Michel Foucault (1926-1984) and Sigmund Freud (1856-1939)*

Since the French post-modernist Michel Foucault relied heavily on the work of Sigmund Freud, we will take a glance at key Freudian concepts before discussing Foucault's postmodernism. Freud was an Austrian physician who developed psychoanalysis. According to Freud, what is essential to human beings is not reason but rather the irrationality that lies behind reason. He named this chaotic jumble of conflicting desires the unconscious in contrast

---

[5] Viktor Frankl refers to the relationship of why and how by quoting Nietzsche who stated, "He who has a *why* to live for can bear with almost any *how*." Viktor E. Frankl, *Man's Search for Meaning* (New York: Pocket Books, 1984), 97.

with the rational, conscious mind. The desires within the unconscious mind are not driven by any rational purpose; they simply are present, wanting fulfillment. One of the most powerful of these drives, argued Freud, is the desire for pleasure, in particular sexual pleasure. Freud thought that it is impossible for human beings to live together in an orderly manner if everyone's aim is only to satisfy their sexual drive for pleasure and to satisfy other drives, including the drives for power, life, and even death.

Since this is the case, argued Freud, this means as people began to live in cities (*civitas* in Latin means city) civilization developed by repressing the drive for life and pleasure and by repressing the drive for the total discharge of life in one intensely exciting moment. This means, according to Freud's logic, civilization, defined as people living together in close proximity in a relatively harmonious manner, is founded upon repression. Repression, though, will cause people to experience inner conflicts that for their health and for the health of civilization as a whole need to be resolved. According to Freud, resolution of inner conflict resulting from repressed desires can occur in psychotherapy sessions. In these sessions, the therapist encourages a patient to unravel his conflicting unconscious desire for life and death by talking freely and without any reservation including on their dreams, which symbolize unconscious unfulfilled desires.⁶

Along with psychotherapy, the negative consequences that repression causes can also be resolved by scientifically understanding the structures of the mind. The more we understand the mind in a scientific manner, argued the atheist Freud, then there will be less of a need to rely upon God to restrain people from acting out violently in order to satisfy their unconscious desires. In Freudian psychology, the mind is divided into three ways: the id, the ego, and the superego. These three regions overlap the conscious mind, the preconscious mind, and the unconscious mind as the diagram below indicates. The id is the region of the unconscious mind that is irrational, impulsive, and pleasure driven. The superego is the region of the mind that is moralistic. Its moral standards are received externally from civilization. The ego acts as an arbitrator, or referee, between the id and the superego.⁷

---

⁶ Sigmund Freud, *Civilization and its Discontents,* trans. James Strachey (New York: W.W Norton & Company, 1961), 51, 66-69, https://archive.org/stream/CivilizationAndItsDiscontents/freud_civilization_and_its_discontents#page/n0/mode/1up/search/id.

⁷ Sigmund Freud, *Beyond the Pleasure Principle*, trans. C.J.M. Hubback (London: International Psycho-analytical Press, MCMXXII), 16-17, 21, 35, https://archive.org/stream/BeyondThePleasurePrinciple_633/freud_sigmund_1856_1939_beyond_the_pleasure_principle#page/n1/mode/1up; Sigmund Freud,

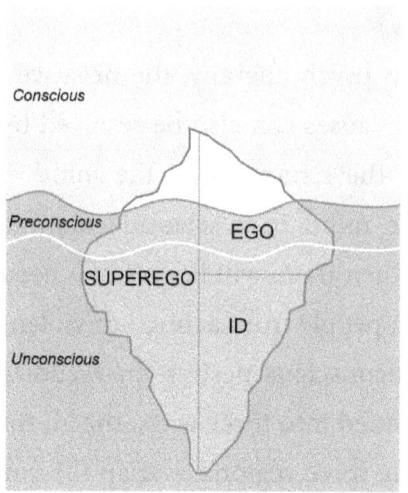

Both with reference to and slight modification of Freud's hypothesis of repression, the French philosopher Michel Foucault, argued that what civilization perceives to be morally bad and morally good is determined by how the civilization chooses to suppress sexual desires by outlawing, or at least perceiving as sinful, certain sexual behavior. Foucault believed that civilization had reached a point where

---

*Civilization and its Discontents* (New York: W.W Norton & Company, 1961), 12-13, 46-54, 74, https://archive.org/stream/CivilizationAndItsDiscontents/freud_civilization_and_its_ discontents#page/n0/mode/1up/search/id, (accessed February 25, 2015); Sigmund Freud, *The Future of an Illusion*, trans. Gregory C. Richter (Buffalo: Broadview Press, 2012), 4, 16-17.

[8] historicair 16:56, 16 December 2006 (UTC), "Diagram of Freud's psyche theory," http://commons.wikimedia.org/wiki/File%3AStructural-Iceberg.svg.

freedom of the individual need not be confined by moral sexual rules imposed upon the individual by society. Tragically, Foucault died of AIDS in 1984.[9]

In profound disagreement with both Freud and Foucault, Christianity as affirmed by St. John Paul II in *Veritatis Splendor* affirms that freedom is not simply defined by the fulfillment of desire but also, and more importantly, by the freedom to act in accordance with our nature given to us by God.[10] Since God created us and since we have the ability to reason in a way animals cannot, our understanding as Christians of what is sexually morally right and morally wrong is not determined by a particular historical context but rather determined by our God-given nature.

As explained by the noted moral theologian Fr. Brian Mullady, Freudian thought, on which Foucault bases his reasoning, understands the moral law in a Kantian manner as an external imposition on human freedom. In contrast, Catholics view the moral law an "interior judgment con-

---

[9] Michel Foucault, *The History of Sexuality: Volume I an Introduction*, trans. Random House (New York: Random House, 1978), 7-10, 15-51.

[10] John Paul II, "Veritatis Splendor," 1993, The Vatican, http://w2.vatican.va/content/john-paul-ii/en/encyclicals/ documents/hf_jp-ii_enc_06081993_veritatis-splendor.html, (accessed April 4, 2015).

cerning our nature"[11] as human beings, specifically on what the various aspects of human nature are oriented to. According to Catholicism, emotions are created by God to naturally follow reason. Therefore, out of reason and not out of fear "I deny my emotions some good that they are seeking because it is leading me to something unreasonable, in other words something that is contrary to my nature."[12] This decision causes my emotional integrity. It does not destroy my emotional integrity. Aristotle also follows this understanding when he describes the intemperate man, the continent man, and the temperate man.[13]

*Jacques Derrida (1930-2004)*

Like Foucault, the French philosopher Jacques Derrida also identified himself with postmodernism's rejection of stable, persistent truth that lasts through history, and with which man has a capacity to bring his mind and actions into correspondence. Unlike Foucault, though, Derrida understood the postmodern claim that all things are fundamentally relative by not focusing on sexuality but rather on language. According to Derrida's understanding of lan-

---

[11] Fr. Brian Mullady, OP, *Theology of the Body* (San Francisco: Shrine of St. Jude Thaddaeus, 200-?), CD 2.

[12] Mullady, *Theology of the Body*, CD 2.

[13] Mullady, *Theology of the Body*, CD 2.

guage it is impossible to know an author's intention because the author lacks an intention even if he claims otherwise. This is because the writings the author produces are shaped by formless desires that are often in conflict with one another. All use of language, argues Derrida, whether written, spoken or thought of, is ambiguous and indeterminate with no underlying message. In order to reveal the meaninglessness behind any use of language, Derrida developed a way of critiquing language called deconstruction. When a person is deconstructing a text in a postmodern manner the purpose is to reveal that what underlies the text is vague, formless and contradictory.[14]

A Christian response to Derrida is that all language has meaning because all language is a participation in the one Word of God, Who is Christ the eternally begotten Word Whom the Father speaks in the love of the Holy Spirit. This

---

[14] John Sallis, *Deconstruction and Philosophy: The Texts of Jacques Derrida* (Chicago: University of Chicago Press, 1987), 6. Sallis in describing deconstruction in a more nuanced manner than I present states, "Now, deconstruction has been explicitly construed by Derrida as an attempt to shake and reinscribe philosophy's endeavor to account by itself for itself by knowledge's systematic and system-forming self-exposition." I interpret this to mean that universal philosophical truths cannot be expressed in language since philosophy cannot, by appealing to itself, validly claim these truths exist. Furthermore, philosophers contradict one another on essential matters.

means that if a person were to truly deconstruct the use of any language, then he will eventually end at the Word that underlies the use of all words. This one Word is Christ who gives ultimate meaning and is the standard by which to judge the truthfulness of words written, spoken, or thought of in any language.[15]

**Post-Modern Action**

The postmodern concepts of the above referred to men, and of similar thinkers, were a factor in bringing about various radical expressions of life as particularly evident by students of the 1960s. The student protests throughout the western world during the tumultuous sixties coincided with what has been called the sexual revolution.[16] We will examine both of these expressions of postmodern thought.

---

[15] For further discussion of the truth of language in relationship to the Trinity see Bruce D. Marshall, *Trinity and Truth* (Cambridge: Cambridge University Press, 2000).

[16] Martin Klimke, *The Other Alliance: Student Protest in West Germany and the United States in the Global Sixties* (Princeton: Princeton University Press, 2010) 1.

## Chapter 12 A Multi-Centric World

*Student Revolts and the 1960s*

The postmodernists' destructive, deconstruction of truth claims was understood by many students of the late 1960s and the 1970s as promising liberation. Liberation, in this context, is understood as liberation from past constraints that once were thought to be in accordance with reality but now, according, to the postmodernists, only impositions of society to maintain order and, to a certain extent, the status quo. Why not, questioned students, forge another path by re-defining what is morally right and wrong, especially when it comes to sexual ethics? In their questioning of authority students in the late 1960s and in the 1970s began holding protests across Europe and in the United states. Below are a few pictures from these protests. Following the photographs is a diagram of the US Kent State University 1970 tragedy where National Guardsmen mistakenly opened fire upon students who were protesting.

296    Western Civilization: Renaissance to Modern Times

*Student 1968 Occupation of France's University of Lyon's Law School*

17

---

[17] GeorgeLouis, "University of Lyon Law School with graffiti June 1968," http://en.wikipedia.org/wiki/File:University_of_Lyon_Law_School_with_graffiti_June_1968.jpg#file. According to Wikimedia commons, "This work is licensed under the Creative Commons Attribution-ShareAlike 3.0 License."

"A female demonstrator offers a flower to military police on guard at the Pentagon during an anti-Vietnam demonstration. Arlington, Virginia, USA." Date 1968.

Below "is a printed map detailing the locations of structures, troop movements, bullet hole locations, and casualties at the Kent State shooting of May 4, 1970."

---

[18] By S.Sgt. Albert R. Simpson. Department of Defense. Department of the Army. Office of the Deputy Chief of Staff for Operations. U.S. Army Audiovisual Center, "Vietnamdem, date 21 October 1967," http://commons.wikimedia.org/wiki/File%3AVietnamdem.jpg.

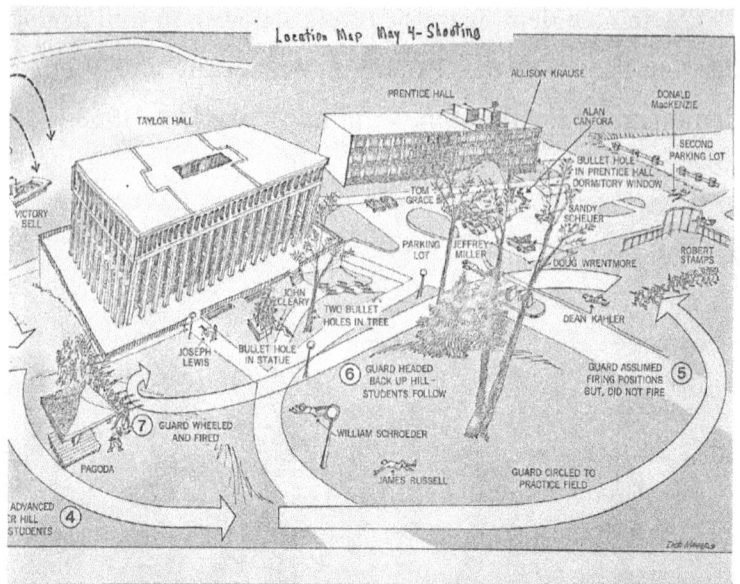

19

A number of the first student protests occurred in West Germany and interestingly involved students studying theology. The reason, as explained by Joseph Ratzinger, was that theology was taught in a highly professional manner that entailed much debate over "historical and structural facts"[20] to the detriment of truths of faith such as whether Christ truly rose from the dead, the immortality of the soul, and the capacity of man to grow spiritually. These theology

---

[19] President (1969-1974 : Nixon). President's Commission on Campus Unrest., "Map of Shootings at Kent State University in 1970," http://commons.wikimedia.org/wiki/File:Map_of_Shootings_at_Kent_State_University_in_1970.jpg.

[20] Joseph Ratzinger, *Church, Ecumenism, & Politics*, trans. Michael J. Miller (San Francisco: Ignatius Press, 1987), 153.

students quickly became "bored with the painstaking professionalism"[21] of their theology teachers and wanted to understand theology as a practical science that would better the world. Unfortunately, many of these students did not look to the saints for inspiration but rather to Karl Marx. In explaining the student mind from this tumultuous time, Ratzinger writes:

> [Many students believed] only Marxism could help an ailing theology back on its feet and restore to it the consciousness of being a real science. On the other hand, only the influx of religious passion and hope could once more lend Marxism, which was already scientifically and politically exhausted, the luster of a bright prospect for humanity outside of its sphere of hegemony.[22]

The wedding of Marxism to theology eventually was expressed in a variety of political theologies. By wedding itself to Marxism, however, argues Ratzinger, theology resembled a blind man being led by a blind man into a

---

[21] Joseph Ratzinger, *Church, Ecumenism, & Politics*, 152.

[22] Joseph Ratzinger, *The Nature and Mission of Theology*, trans. Adrian Walker (San Francisco: Ignatius Press, 1995), 79.

ditch.²³ In describing theology students influenced by Marxist thought, Ratzinger refers to a flyer issued in the summer of 1969 by Protestant theology students of the University of Tubingen. The flyer asserted that "The New Testament is a document of inhumanity, a large-scale deception of the masses."²⁴ The flyer went on, describes Ratzinger, to accuse "the Church of sharing in the guilt of capitalist exploitation of the poor, and it ascribed to traditional theology the function of propping up the system."²⁵

**The Sexual Revolution**

Students were not the only ones who questioned authority and traditional ways of perceiving morality, education, governments, military, and other like realities. A common subject which people of all age groups questioned in a particularly intense manner during the 1960s and 1970s was traditional sexual morality. The French, female postmodern, existentialist writer Simone de Beauvoir (1908-1986), and longtime friend of the French existentialist philosopher Jean-Paul Sartre, concisely represented this

---

[23] Ratzinger, *The Nature and Mission of Theology*, 79.

[24] Joseph Ratzinger, *Salt of the Earth*, trans. Adrian Walker (San Francisco: Ignatius Press, 1997), 77.

[25] Ratzinger, *Salt of the Earth*, 77.

questioning in her 1949 book, *The Second Sex*.[26] According to Simone de Beauvoir, a person "is not born a woman but rather becomes a woman."[27] This is because sex is what one is born with, but gender, a term that Beauvoir did not use but that clarifies her ideas, defined by what is male, what is female, and what is between male and female, is cultural.[28] As she explains, "No biological, psychic, or economic destiny defines the figure that the human female takes on in society; it is civilization as a whole that elaborates this intermediary product between the male and the eunuch that is called feminine."[29]

Along with the influence of postmodern existential thought, there were other factors that helped to cause this questioning. A main one was the advancement of technology. As technology developed, more and more countries began transitioning from agriculturally-based economies to factory- and office-based economies. In agriculturally-based economies, children had significant economic value since they can be put to work on the farm at little cost. However, in a factory- and office-based economy that re-

---

[26] Deirdre Bair, *Simone de Beauvoir: A Biography* (New York: Simon & Schuster, 1990), 179-182.

[27] Simone de Beauvoir, *The Second Sex*, trans. Constance Borde and Sheila Malovany (New York: Random House, 2010), 283.

[28] de Beauvoir, *The Second Sex*, xviii.

[29] de Beauvoir, *The Second Sex*, 283.

stricts child labor, children have much less economic value since they cannot be as easily put to work by their parents as they were in the past. This means that as a country develops its economy by relying more on technology, there is less of a financial incentive, in the sense of profit, for men and women to raise a number of children and even to restrain their sexual desires in order to keep their family unit intact. One negative side effect of couples having only one, a few or even no children at all is that there will be few if any family members to care for the couple when they are elderly.[30]

It is not surprising, therefore, that during the 1960s birth control devices began to be used with ever greater frequencies, and colleges/universities instituted co-ed interaction including in dormitories. As the bonding aspect of sexual intercourse became separated more and more from the generative aspect, in other words being open to babies, the next logical step occurred. If men and women can separate the sexual union from the end of giving birth to babies, some argued, then there is nothing wrong with men having sex with men and women having sex with women. In all three cases, what is being sought is sexual union with another human being while not being open to new life. During the 1970s, consequently, the gay liberation movement

---

[30] Alvin J. Schmidt, *Veiled and Silenced: How Culture Shaped Sexist Theology* (Macon: Mercer University Press, 1989), 35.

developed and began to demand legal protection. The logic of separating sexual union from procreation was also evident in the rise of pornography. In 1953, the US publisher Hugh Hefner with his journal *Playboy* effectively marketed pornography to the "average" man. Currently, the selling of pornography is a multibillion dollar industry.[31]

**Postmodernism Architecture**

How we choose to construct the buildings we live is an indicator of our world views, our philosophies, and our theological beliefs. For example, the soaring, majestic medieval and renaissance cathedrals physically represent the then common belief in God and transcendent realities, such as angels, heaven, purgatory, and hell. Our current postmodern age also has its own unique architecture that represents the inner conviction of many that ultimately there is no stable truth and no philosophical and religious principles that stay true as time changes. As evident below, postmodern architecture represents the postmodern relativism by its lack of a clearly delineated form. For this reason, when one looks at a postmodern building it is very difficult to determine what its purpose is.[32]

---

[31] Gavin Lewis, *WCIV Volume 2: Since 1300 Student Edition* (Boston: Wadsworth, 2012), 554

[32] Lewis, *WCIV Volume 2: Since 1300 Student Edition*, 566.

San Antonio Public Library, Texas

Front of the Museum the *Neue Staatgalerie* in Stuttgart, Germany

---

[33] Zereshk, "San Antonio Public Library," photograph, http://commons.wikimedia.org/wiki/File%3ASAPL3.jpg.

## Quiz 11 for Chapter 11

1-4. With respect to truth, define postmodernism.

5-7. Describe the postmodernism of Jean-François Lyotard in relationship to metanarratives. First, define what a metanarrative is. Then state what Lyotard thought about metanarratives.

8. State Michel Foucault's postmodernism in relationship to sexuality.

---

[34] Mussklprozz, "Front of the Neue Staatgalerie Stuttgart, 1984," http://commons.wikimedia.org/wiki/File%3A Staatsgaleriel.jpg.

9-11. State Jacques Derrida's postmodernism by referring to his deconstructionism.




12-13. List two ways by which postmodern thought was expressed.

    12.

    13.


18-19. Name two key characteristics of postmodern architecture

    18.

    19.

# Chapter 12

## A Multi-Centric World

**Introduction**

Mikhail Gorbachev's resignation and subsequent dissolution of the Soviet Union in 1991 signaled the end of a bi-polar world divided between the two superpowers of the United States of America and the Soviet Union. For a while, the US acted as the sole superpower in the world, but as the influence of the US began to slowly wane, multiple, competing centers of world power became stronger. These include, but are not limited to, the European Union, Eurasian Economic Union, India, the "Asian Tiger" countries, China, and Brazil. The first two mentioned are roughly based on the Cold War divisions in Western Europe and Eurasia. The tension between East and West is much more subtle now than it was during the Cold War and may not be as much of a concern to world stability in comparison to other regions, in particular the Middle East and parts of Africa. These regions have and are producing terrorists who have committed horrendous acts throughout the world.

One intergovernmental organization that has tried to

maintain world peace in the midst of sporadic terrorist activity is the United Nations (UN). The UN was founded in 1945 to ensure another World War will not occur. Since the UN lacks an effective military force of its own to enforce its decisions, at times it has proven to be ineffective in resolving world conflicts. Perhaps such a lack is for the best since if the UN had an effective military force comparable to or better than any other military force, it might become controlled by people intent on ruling the entire world in a dictatorial manner.

Some hope that world harmony will be attained as western countries promote global prosperity promised by capitalism. This promotion has been called globalization. Such people claim that although capitalism involves negative effects of competition, in which the losers suffer consequences, when taken as a whole capitalism has consistently raised the standard of living for all. Others contend that this would be true if international trade was done in a fair, free manner and did not occur at the expense of the environment or involve sweatshops known for their unjust practices to workers.

Those who protest globalization point out that western countries have consistently protected their own banks, farms, and industries with subsidies and tariffs in order to maintain their status as superpowers. One very evident example is the so-called "Washington Consensus" that promotes globalization according to principles established by

US-influenced organizations (The US Treasury, the World Bank, and the International Monetary Fund).[1] This raises the question as to whether the western dominated approach to politics and economics is the only viable option. If it is not, what are the other options? With a hope to more objectively understand the phenomena of western-dominated globalization, we will take a look at a number of the various centers of power located both in the west and the east. These new centers of power are promoting what Narcís Serra and Joseph E. Stiglitz describe as "a post-Washington Consensus."[2]

**European Union**

One economic reason why the European Union was founded was for western European countries to collectively compete with the super power status of the United States. It was founded in 1992 by the Treaty of Maastricht shortly after the Soviet Union was dissolved in 1991. As evident below, according to the Treaty, the goals of the European Union are to establish a common European citizenship, a

---

[1] Narcís Serra and Joseph E. Stiglitz, *The Washington Consensus Reconsidered: Towards a New Global Governance* (Oxford: Oxford University Press, 2008), 3-5.

[2] Serra and Stiglitz, *The Washington Consensus Reconsidered : Towards a New Global Governance*, 12.

common currency, a common social policy, a common economic policy, a common foreign policy, and a common security policy.

*The Maastricht Treaty on European Union February 7, 1992*

> Resolved to mark a new stage in the process of European integration undertaken with the establishment of the European Communities,
> 
> Recalling the historic importance of the ending of the division of the European continent and the need to create firm bases for the construction of the future Europe,
> 
> Confirming their attachment to the principles of liberty, democracy and respect for human rights and fundamental freedoms and of the rule of law,
> 
> Desiring to deepen the solidarity between their peoples while respecting their history, their culture and their traditions,
> 
> Desiring to enhance further the democratic and efficient functioning of the institutions so as to enable them better to carry out, within a single institutional framework, the tasks entrusted to the,
> 
> Resolved to achieve the strengthening and

the convergence of their economies and to establish an economic and monetary union including, in accordance with the provision of this Treaty, a single and stable currency,

Determined to promote economic and social progress for their peoples, with the context of the accomplishment of the internal market and of reinforced cohesion and environmental protection, and to implement policies ensuring that advances in economic integration are accompanied by parallel progress in other fields,

Resolved to establish a citizenship common to nationals of their countries,

Resolved to implement a common foreign and security policy including the eventual framing of a common defense policy, which might in time lead to a common defense, thereby reinforcing the European identity and its independence in order to promote peace, security and progress in Europe and in the world,

Reaffirming their objective to facilitate the free movement of persons, while ensuring the safety and security of their peoples, by including provisions on justice and home affairs in this Treaty.

> Resolved to continue to process of creating an ever closer union among the peoples of Europe, in which decisions are taken as closely as possible to the citizen in accordance with the principle of subsidiarity.
>
> In view of further steps to be taken in order to advance European integration,
>
> Have decided to establish a European Union and to this end have designated as their plenipotentiaries.[3]

As the European Union continues to incorporate more member states, it has faced a number of critical questions. Is the granting of European Union membership to countries that are not considered economically advanced, such as the Ukraine, in the best interest of the European Union as a whole? Will these countries de-stabilize the European Union? Similarly, will the granting of European Union membership to countries that have significant religious difference from the vast majority of European countries put the entire union at risk of disintegrating? One example is Turkey, which in 1987 applied for accession to the predecessor of the European Union called the European Eco-

---

[3] Casey Michel, "The Maastricht Treaty," Eurotreaties, http://www.eurotreaties.com/maastrichteu.pdf.

nomic Union.[4] In 1999, the European Union officially recognized Turkey as a candidate for full membership.[5]

In 2004, Cardinal Joseph Ratzinger argued in France's magazine *Le Figaro* that bringing Turkey into the European Union jeopardizes European culture since "Europe is a cultural and not a geographical continent." Turkey, asserted Ratzinger, "always represented another continent throughout history, in permanent contrast with Europe, so to equate the two continents would be a mistake." In order for the European Union to stay intact, Ratzinger believes, it must acknowledge and maintain its Christian roots.[6]

**Eurasian Economic Union**

A few of the Eurasian countries have taken Russia's lead to form a competing union called the Eurasian Economic Union. Similar to the goals of the European Union, the Eurasian Economic Union was formed on May 29th, 2014, to integrate the economic markets of various Eura-

---

[4] Yonah Alexander, Edgar H. Brenner, and Serhat Tutuncuoglu Krause, *Turkey: Terrorism, Civil Rights, and the European Union* (New York: Routledge, 2008), 229-233.

[5] Alexander, Brenner, and Krause, *Turkey: Terrorism, Civil Rights, and the European Union*, 401.

[6] "Ratzinger on Turkey in EU, European Secularism," Catholic Culture, http://www.catholicculture.org/news/features/ index.cfm?recnum=31436.

sian countries. As of 2015, the member states only include Russia, Belarus, Kazakhstan, and Armenia.[7] Like Turkey, and unlike the other three countries of the other Eurasian Economic Union, Kazakhstan is predominantly an Islamic country. Whether this will be a destabilizing factor in the Eurasian Economic Union remains to be determined.

[8]

## India

---

[7] "Eurasian Economic Union," EAEU, http://www.eaeunion.org/?lang=en#about; "How Significant Is the Eurasian Economic Union?" *The Diplomat*, http://thediplomat.com/2014/06/how-significant-is-the-eurasian-economic-union/.

[8] Presidential Press and Information Office, "Member states of the Customs Union and the Single Economic Space," map, http://commons.wikimedia.org/wiki/File%3AMember_states_of_the_Customs_Union_and_the_Single_Economic_Space.png.

In the 1980s into the 1990s, India's economy rapidly grew after it shifted from being a command-based economy, determined by state policy, to a market-based economy. A market-based economy is essentially determined by privately-owned companies competing for customers. The market reforms were solidified in 1991 when India's Finance Minister and economist, Dr. Manmohan Singh, began systematically to implement economic reforms.[9]

The economic reforms that were undertaken by India that led to its economic growth included tax reforms, deregulation, allowing foreign investors greater access, and privatization of state-owned industries.[10] In 2013, India was ranked the fourth largest economy of the world, according to GDP, behind the United States, the European Union, and China.[11] It is also one of the fastest growing economies in the world.[12] While India's industrial output, foreign investment, and export sectors all have indicated growth after

---

[9] Bishwa Nath Sigh, Mohan Prasad Shrivastava, and Narendra Prasad, *Economic Reforms in India* (New Delhi: APH Publishing Corporation, 2003), 75.

[10] Sigh, Shrivastava, & Prasad, *Economic Reforms in India*, 47-48, 76.

[11] "India, Country Comparison GDP," CIA, The World Fact Book, https://www.cia.gov/library/publications/the-world-factbook/rankorder/2001rank.html?countryname=India&countrycode=in&regionCode=sas&rank=4#in.

[12] Sigh, Shrivastava, & Prasad, *Economic Reforms in India*, 77.

the reforms were made, these advances occurred at the same time when India's poverty and unemployment were increasing.[13]

**Asian Tigers**

Asia's high economically performing nations and one region, which were first designated as the Asian Tigers, are Hong Kong, Singapore, South Korea, and Taiwan. Others include Indonesia, Malaysia, and Thailand. Similar to India, after the Asian Tigers underwent a phase of industrialization during the 1960s through the 1990s, while reforming their economies in accordance with a market-based approach in place of a command economy, they experienced a steady and high growth rate.[14] As detailed by Thomas M. Leonard, the common characteristics of the East Asian Tigers were to:

> focus on exports to rich industrialized nations, sustained rate of double-digit growth for decades, non-democratic and relatively authoritarian political systems during the early years, high

---

[13] Sigh, Shrivastava, & Prasad, *Economic Reforms in India*, 70-71.

[14] Thomas M. Leonard, *Encyclopedia of the Developing World Volume I, A-E* (New York: Routledge, 2006), 816.

tariffs on imports, undervalued national currencies, trade surplus, and a high savings rate.[15]

A common inherent weakness in their approach, again pointed out by Leonard, was their overreliance on demand for what the Asian Tiger countries could export.[16] An interesting feature in the Asian Tiger's success story is their combination of economic freedom with a political authoritarian system. This demonstrates that at least elements of capitalism's free market approach can be combined with dictatorial systems. It is not intrinsically necessary for the economic model of capitalism to be integrated with a political system of democracy. It also effectively works in authoritarian regimes.

**China**

As mentioned previously, the major economic, political and military power of China blends together a capitalistic market based approach to its economy, with an authoritarian socialist, also called communist, political system. Under Deng Xiaoping's leadership, beginning in 1998,

---

[15] Thomas M. Leonard, *Encyclopedia of the Developing World* Volume I, A-E (New York: Routledge, 2006), 816.

[16] Leonard, *Encyclopedia of the Developing World* Volume I, A-E, 816.

China moved away from a state-owned, directed economy that Mao Zedong (1893-1976) had established. Deng Xiaoping did this by dissolving collective farms, permitting families to own land, privatizing certain state-owned industries, encouraging the formation of privately-owned companies, and by inviting foreign investors into China.[17] Also under Deng Xiaoping's leadership, the communist party's constitution was reworded. According to the revision, China is a "socialist market economy."[18] To view Deng Xiaoping's impact on the economic vitality of China, measured by GDP, see the chart below.

China exhibits its totalitarian socialist side by not allowing its currency, the Yuan, to be determined by supply of and demand for the Yuan. Instead, the government sets their currency at an artificially lower rate in relationship to other currencies, above all with the US currency. This allows China to sell goods at a very low price in the US and in other countries while at the same time ensuring that imported goods into China sell at a higher price than they would be if the Chinese Yuan was not artificially deval-

---

[17] Patricia Buckley Ebrey, *The Cambridge Illustrated History of China*, Second Edition (Cambridge: Cambridge University Press, 2010), 333.

[18] Patricia Buckley Ebrey, *The Cambridge Illustrated History of China*, Second Edition, 336.

ued.[19]

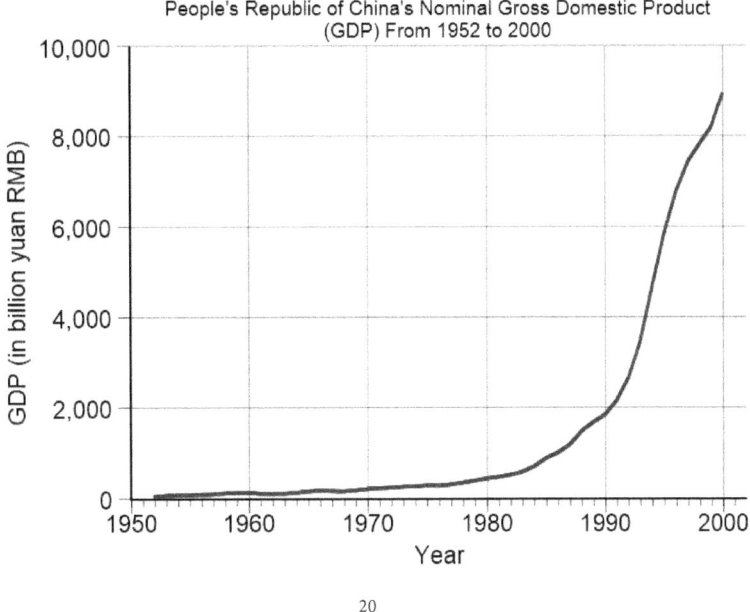

[20]

The devaluing of the currency is an example of an authoritarian economic practice that reflects China's political authoritarian communism. Another notable example of China's communist state limiting freedom, in this case political freedom, occurred on June 4th, 1989, when the government violently opposed a pro-democracy movement

---

[19] Wayne M. Morrison, and Jonathan E. Sanford, *China's Currency and Economic Issues* (New York: Nova Science Publishers, 2006), 4-5.

[20] Delphi234, "GDP of China in RMB from 1952 to 2000," http://commons.wikimedia.org/wiki/File%3AGDP_of_China_in_RMB_from_1952_to_2000.svg.

that was gathered together at Tiananmen Square. It is not clear how many protesters were killed by governmental forces at Tiananmen Square. According to the Chinese government, 241 protestors were killed. According to the Soviet Union 10,000 protestors were killed, and according to the Chinese Red Cross, 2,600 protestors were killed.[21]

**Brazil**

We will now turn our attention to a former colony of Portugal that is now the most powerful country in Latin America, Brazil. This democratic country is the fifth largest country in the world and has sustained consistent economic growth. In 2013, the economic ranking determined by GDP was as follows: 1. United States, 2. European Union, 3. China, 4. India, 5. Japan, 6. Germany, 7. Russia, 8. Brazil.[22] Other economic data indicate that Brazil is the world's third largest exporter of food, has been recently ranked, in 2010, as the sixth in world manufacturing power, and may, due to recent discoveries, become a major exporter of oil.

---

[21] Andrew Langley, *Tiananmen Square: Massacre Crushes China's Democracy Movement* (Mankato: Compass Point Books, 2009), 16.

[22] "Country Comparison: GDP (purchasing power parity)," CIA Factbook, https://www.cia.gov/library/publications/the-world-factbook/rankorder/2001rank.html?countryname= Brazil&countrycode=br&regionCode=soa&rank=8#br.

Even though Brazil is rich in oil, half of its cars do not run on gasoline but rather on a fuel derived from sugar cane called ethanol.[23]

A main reason for Brazil's economic success is traceable to the late 1980s when the government began transforming the country's economy on a competitive market-based model. Taxes on imports and exports were greatly reduced, and the government, while retaining some companies, sold off others worth $110 billion. For this reason Brazil was called the "privatization's poster child."[24]

**Africa**

The book *Asian Tigers, African Lions* asks the question, "Why are there Asian tigers, but no African lions."[25] In other words, why is it that "Sub-Saharan African countries since independence have not become richer while countries

---

[23] Michael Reid, *Brazil: The Troubled Rise of a Global Power* (New Haven, CT: Yale University Press, 2014), 5.

[24] Lael Brainard, and Leonardo Martinez-Diaz, *Brazil As an Economic Superpower? Understanding Brazil's Changing Role in the Global Economy* (Harrisonburg: The Brookings Institution, 2009), 6.

[25] Bernard Berendsen, Ton Dietz, H G C Schulte Nordholt, and Roel van der Veen, *Asian Tigers: African Lions: Comparing the Development Performance of Southeast Asian and Africa* (Leiden: Brill, 2013), 3.

in Southeast Asia have?"²⁶ With the purpose of answering this question, in 2006 a research project was founded and funded by the Netherlands Minister for Development Cooperation. One explanation that was offered by this research project was that the Southeast Asian countries which have experienced rapid economic improvement were, from the perspective of the whole, economically stable. In addition, farmers and people desiring to begin small businesses were granted economic freedom, and the Asian government aided the poor and those living in rural areas.²⁷ These three simultaneously occurring factors precipitated in the Asian countries' economic "turning points" during which their countries entered into a phase of transition from "continuous poverty to sustained growth."²⁸

According to the above theory, unless African countries fulfill the three mentioned pre-conditions, they will remain in a continuous state of poverty. Below is a map that illustrates Africa's low economic development in comparison with the rest of the world. Compare Africa with India, China, and the Asian Tiger Countries. If you need help in identifying the Asian countries please see the second map.

---

[26] Berendsen, et alia, *Asian Tigers: African Lions*, 3.

[27] Berendsen, et alia, *Asian Tigers: African Lions*, 12.

[28] Berendsen, et alia, *Asian Tigers: African Lions*, 13.

Chapter 12 A Multi-Centric World 323

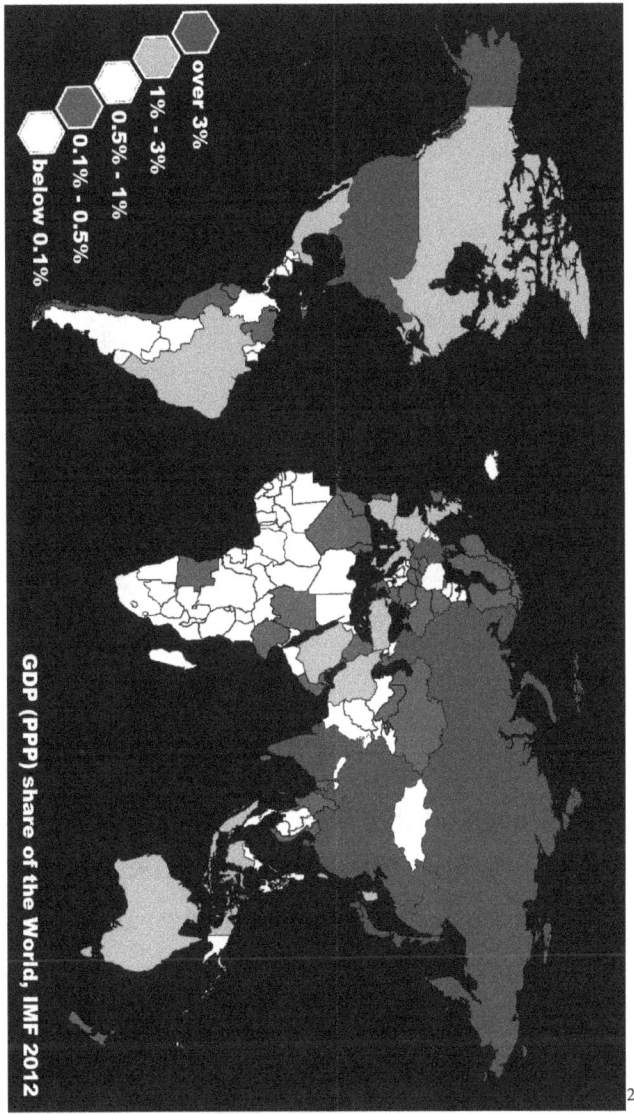

[29] Quandanda, "Gross domestic product based on purchasing-power-parity (PPP) share of world total in 2012 imf," http://commons.wikimedia.org/wiki/File%3AShare_of_world_gdp_2012_imf.png.

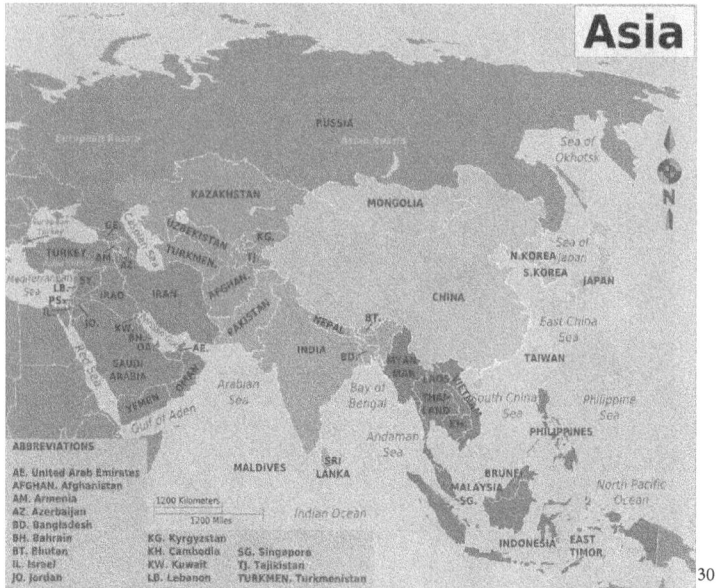

## Conclusion

We have come to the end of our survey of Western civilization. Throughout this overview, the relationship of the many to the one has been a consistently recurring theme. Can the many people, of many nations live harmoniously as one global family? Will the European Union and Eurasian Economic Union, which strives to respect diversity in unity, last? If so, what are the ideal conditions that will assure its survival, and what are conditions that will likely lead to its

---

[30] Travelpleb, "A draft new map for use on Wikivoyage," http://commons.wikimedia.org/wiki/File%3AMap_of_Asia_draft.png.

collapse and possibly another major war? Will one nation or empire work toward eliminating other weaker nations, such as France under Napoleon, Germany under Hitler, the USSR under Stalin, in order to achieve an oppressive totalitarian unity? As we end this book, may we think about what we have learned about Western Civilization from the relationship of the one to the many. What can we do to ensure that the legitimate diversity present in western civilization as it interacts with the diversity present in non-western civilizations will not be a cause for strife and war but rather as a reason for ever deeper unity?

**Quiz 12 for Chapter 12**

1-3. Do you think that the United Nations, or similar intergovernmental organization, should be granted an effective military force comparable to or better than the militaries of the major world powers?

1.

2.

3.

4-6. First, define globalization. Then, point out negative and positive aspects caused by globalization.

    4.

    5.

    6.

7-10. With respect to economic performance, and in reference to chapter 12, compare and contrast Africa with the South East Asian countries known as the Asian Tigers.

# Index

Able Archer .................................................................. 253, 273
Abstract Art ................................................. 163, 184, 186, 190
Adam Smith.............................................................. 143-45, 255
Albert Bierstadt ........................................................................ 80
Allies ..................... 174-75, 196-97, 205, 209, 219, 222-23, 250
American Declaration of Independence ..................... 51, 52, 54
André Breton ....................................................................... 212
André Derain ....................................................................... 181
Angelo de Giudici ........................................................... 187-88
Anne-Louis Trioson ............................................................... 82
appeasement ..................................................... 216, 218, 220
Archimedes ............................................................................ 29
Aristarchus........................................................................ 29-30
Aristotle...................................................... 38-9, 281, 292
Asian Tiger................................................ 307, 316-317, 321-22
Austro-Hungarian Empire .................... 108-09, 163, 174-75
Axis powers......................... 204-05, 216, 221, 224, 258, 250
barocco .................................................................................. 14
Batista ................................................................................ 269
Battle of Agincourt................................................................. 10
Battle of Castillon.................................................................. 11
Battle of Hastings .................................................................... 2
Bay of Pigs........................................................................... 269
Benjamin Latrobe............................................................... 44-5
Berlin Crisis ................................................................ 253, 268
Bernini ................................................................... 14-6, 18
Big Bang ............................................................................. 246

327

Bill of Rights ................................................................ 7, 52
Bismarck ........................................... 97, 99, 104-05, 201
Blackshirts ...................................................................... 207
Boston Tea party ............................................................. 50
Canova ......................................................................... 43-4
capitalism ........................... 142, 144, 249, 253-57, 308, 317
Caravaggio .................................................................. 17-8
Casper David Friedrich .................................................. 78
Castro ............................................................................ 269
Cavour ........................................................................... 103
Center Party ................................................................... 99
Cézanne .............................................................. 117, 121-22
Charles I ..................................................................... 5-6, 13
Christopher Columbus ............................................. 142-43
Coercive Acts .................................................................. 50
Cold War ........ 234, 249, 253, 260, 266-68, 271, 273-74, 276, 281, 307
Communism ............................... 209-10, 212, 254, 256-57, 271
Concert of Europe ......................................................... 108
Congo ....................................................................... 165-68
Congress of Vienna ................................................ 102-03, 107
Continental System ......................................................... 94
Copernicus ................................................... 25, 28-9, 32-6
Courbet ..................................................................... 147-49
Cuban missile crisis ............................................ 253, 269-270
Cubism .......................................................................... 184
Dada .............................................................................. 188
Daumier ................................................................. 153-155
David Ben-Gurion ......................................................... 265
De Stijl ...................................................................... 189-90
Declaration of the Rights of Man ................................... 60
Degas ........................................................................ 116-17
Delacroix ........................................................................ 88
Deng Xiaoping .......................................................... 317-18

# Index

Derrida .................................................................. 285, 292-93
Descartes ........................................................................ 26-7
Die Brücke ..................................................................... 181-83
Directory ...................................................................... 61, 70-1
Eastern Master Plan ............................................................ 204
Edward VI .......................................................................... 4
Einstein ........................................................................ 245-46
Elizabeth I ......................................................................... 4
Emile Nolde ..................................................................... 183
Enabling Act ..................................................................... 200
Engels ............................................................... 145, 256, 259
Enrico Fermi ..................................................................... 240
Entente Powers ................................................... 108-09, 174-75
Ernest Rutherford ........................................................... 238-39
Ernst Ludwig Kirchner ...................................................... 182
European Union ........................ 307, 309-10, 312-13, 315, 320, 324
Expressionism ..................................... 118, 163, 176-77, 179, 181
Faraday ............................................................................ 242
fascism ..................................................................... 207-09, 254
Fat Man ............................................................................ 231
Fauvism ............................................................................ 179
Feuillants ............................................................................ 67
Final Solution ................................................................ 202-03
Five Year Plan ................................................................... 211
Foucault ............................................................ 285, 287, 290-92
Fourteen Points ................................................................. 215
Fragonard .......................................................................... 21
Francis Bacon .................................................................. 27-8
Francis Collins .................................................................. 245
Francis Crick ................................................................. 243-44
Franz Ferdinand ................................................................ 175
Franz Marc ........................................................................ 179
Frederic Edwin Church ....................................................... 81

French Revolution ......... 1, 13, 49, 57-8, 61-4, 67-72, 88, 91-100, 137
Freud ............................................................................. 211, 285, 287-91
Futurism .................................................................................... 186
Galen ....................................................................................... 39-40
Galilei .................................................................... 25, 31, 35-7
Gallicanism ................................................................................ 13
Garibaldi ................................................................................. 103
Gauguin ............................................................................ 117, 120
General Will ....................................................................... 57-60
Gentileschi ................................................................................ 18
George Washington ............................................................... 52
Georges Braque ..................................................................... 184
German Empire ............................... 98, 108, 163, 174-75, 195
Girondins ................................................................................. 67
Glorious Revolution ................................................................. 6
Gorbachev ............................................................. 249, 275, 307
Göring ............................................................................ 222, 226
Goya ......................................................................................... 85
Greek civil war ....................................................................... 271
Guild ............................................................................... 137, 139
guilds ................................................................................ 136-42
Hannah Arendt ....................................................................... 57
Heisenberg ..................................................................... 236, 241
Henry Ford .................................................................. 128-29, 132
Henry Fuseli ............................................................................ 83
Henry V .................................................................................... 10
Henry VII ................................................................................... 3
Henry VIII ................................................... 3, 132, 136, 141
Himmler ............................................................... 202-05, 222-23
Hiroshima ........................................... 216, 224, 231-32, 241
Hitler ................... 198-202, 205-06, 215-220, 223, 226, 228, 325
Hobbes .................................................................................... 49
Holocaust .............................................................................. 202

# Index

House of York ............................................................................... 3
Hugh Hefner ........................................................................... 303
Human Genome Project ...................................................... 245
Hundred Years War .......................................................... 10-11
Imperialism ........................................................ 163-64, 170, 172
Impressionism ..................... 91, 109-10, 116-17, 123, 177
Industrial Revolution .. 109, 127-28, 131-34, 141-47, 158, 163-64, 255
International Monetary Fund ............................................ 309
Interregnum ............................................................................. 6
invisible hand ......................................................... 145, 255-56
Isaac Newton ...................................... 25, 37-9, 243, 245
Jacobins ................................................................................... 67
Jacques Necker .................................................................... 63
Jacques-Louis David ........................................................... 41
James Clerk Maxwell ....................................................... 242
James II ................................................................................. 6-7
James VI .................................................................................. 5
James Watson ..................................................................... 243
Joan of Arc .................................................................... 10-11
John Constable .................................................................... 76
John Paul II ................................................................. 237, 291
Kanagawa Treaty ................................................................ 172
Kant ............................................................................... 281, 291
Kepler ............................................................................ 25, 35-7
Khnopff ................................................................................ 159
Khrushchev ......................................................................... 270
King Leopold ................................................................. 165-68
Korean War ................................................................. 253, 263
Kulturkampf .......................................................................... 98
League of Nations ........................................................ 215-18
Legislative Assembly ........................................... 61, 65, 67
Lemaitre ............................................................................... 246
Lenin ............................................................................ 210, 259-60

Liberalism ..... 144
Little Boy ..... 231
Livy ..... 41
Locke ..... 49, 53-7
Louis XI ..... 11
Louis XIV ..... 12-3
Louis XVI ..... 1, 13, 61-2, 68, 95-6
Louis XVIII ..... 95-6
Luddites ..... 136
Lyotard ..... 285-86
Magna Carta ..... 2, 5
Manet ..... 112-13
Mao Zedong ..... 318
Marcel Duchamp ..... 188
Marco Polo ..... 168
Marie Antoinette ..... 1, 13, 68
Marie Curie ..... 238
Marx ..... 145, 256-57, 259, 299
Mary I ..... 4
*Matisse* ..... 180
Matthew C. Perry ..... 172
Max Weber ..... 133
Mazzini ..... 102-03
Mendel ..... 243
mercantilism ..... 142-43
Metternich ..... 91, 105-07
Michelangelo ..... 15-18
Millet ..... 150-52
Molotov-Ribbentrop pact ..... 249, 252
Mondrian ..... 189-90
Monet ..... 110-11, 113, 117
Montesquieu ..... 49, 53, 56
Mujahedeen ..... 272-73

Index

Munch .................................................................................... 178
Mussolini ................................................................. 105, 207, 209
Nagasaki .................................................... 216, 231-32, 241
Napoleon Bonaparte ............... 85, 91-6, 98, 100, 102, 106-7, 222, 325
nation state ................................................................. 92-3, 144
National Constituent Assembly ...................................... 61, 64
National Convention ......................................................... 61, 67-8
Nazis ........................................... 198, 202-3, 207, 222-23, 225
neoclassical ................................................................. 25, 41, 44
Neo-Classicalism ............................................................. 109
Neville Chamberlain ....................................................... 215-20
Newton ............................................................. 25, 37-9, 243, 245
Nicholas II ........................................................................ 210
Niels Bohr ....................................................................... 239
Oliver Cromwell .................................................................. 6
opium ............................................................ 168-69, 172-73
Opium War ................................................................. 168-69
Osama bin Laden ............................................................ 272
Ottoman Empire ......................................................... 174-176
Papal States .................................................................. 100, 104
Paul von Hindenburg ..................................................... 199-201
Pearl Harbor ................................................................... 222
Picasso ............................................................................ 185
Pissarro ........................................................................... 113
Pius XI ................................................................... 105, 209
Pointillism ...................................................................... 123
postmodern ............................................... 282-87, 292-95
President Hoover ............................................................ 198
primeval atom ................................................................ 246
Ptolemy ............................................................................ 31
Quadragesimo Anno ....................................................... 209
Quadruple Alliance ........................................................ 107
Quantum theory ............................................................. 242

Ratzinger .................................. 131-32, 223, 235-36, 298-300, 313
Reagan ................................................................................ 272
Realism ................................................... 109, 146, 148, 158
Reichstag Fire Decree ........................................... 99, 199-200
Reign of Terror ................................................................. 69-70
Renoir ................................................................... 114-15, 117
Richard Cromwell ..................................................................... 6
Richard III ............................................................................... 3
Richelieu ............................................................................... 12
Robespierre ...................................................................... 69-71
Rococo ........................................................................... 21, 41
Romanticism .............................................................. 71-2, 109
Rousseau ................................................................ 49, 57-9, 72
Russo-Japanese War ..................................................... 173, 209
Sartre ................................................................................. 300
Schwabe ............................................................................. 158
Seurat ......................................................................... 117, 123
Shoah ................................................................................ 202
Simone de Beauvoir ........................................................ 300-01
Sixth Coalition ............................................................. 95-6, 100
Smith .................................................................... 143-5, 255-6
socialism ........................................... 142, 145-46, 207, 209, 255-57
Soviet .... 195, 210-11, 221-25, 228, 234, 249-53, 259-63, 266-76, 279,
 ................................................................................. 307, 309
Soviet Afghan war ........................................................... 274-75
Soviet Blockade in Berlin ........................................... 253, 260
Soviet war in Afghanistan ..................................................... 253
Spinning Mule ................................................................ 128-29
St. Benedict's rule ........................................................... 140-41
Stalin .......................................... 210-11, 216, 228, 249, 260, 325
Stamp Act ............................................................................ 50
Stuarts ................................................................................... 3
Sudetenland .................................................................. 218-19

# Index

Suez Crisis .................................................................. 253, 265
Supremacy Act ................................................................... 4
Surrealism ....................................................... 195, 211-12
Symbolism ......................................................... 14, 127, 158
Tennis Court Oath ............................................................ 63
The Green Folder ........................................................... 222
Théodore Géricault ........................................................ 86-7
Thomas Cole .................................................................... 79
Thomas Gainsborough .................................................... 76-7
Thomas H. Morgan ........................................................ 243
Treaty of Amity and Commerce ...................................... 172
Treaty of Maastricht ....................................................... 309
Triple Alliance ..................................................... 108-09, 174
Tudor ............................................................................. 3-5
Turner ............................................................................ 74-5
Tycho Brahe ............................................................. 25, 34-35
Umberto Boccioni ........................................................... 186
United Nations ................................... 250-51, 265, 267, 308
Urban VIII ....................................................................... 37
US Constitution .............................................................. 52
US Treasury ................................................................... 309
Vasnetsov ....................................................................... 160
Velázquez ........................................................................ 20
Versailles Treaty ........................................................ 196-97
Victor Emanuel II .......................................................... 103
Vietnam War ........................................................ 253, 271-72
Vincent Van Gogh .......................................................... 117
War Guilt clause ............................................................ 196
War in Afghanistan ............................... 253, 272-73, 275
War in the Vendee ........................................................... 71
War of the Roses .............................................................. 3
Weimar Republic ........................................................... 196
Wilhelm Leibl ................................................................ 157

William Blake .................................................................................83-4
William Harvey ...........................................................25, 39-40
William II............................................................................... 196
William III of Orange................................................................ 7
William the Conqueror ..................................................... 2, 10
Winslow Homer................................................................... 156
Winston Churchill .................................... 216, 220-21, 252
Woodrow Wilson .....................................................175, 215, 217
World Bank .......................................................................... 309
World War I .................................................107-109, 163-65, 173-6
World Wide Web.................................................................. 234
Yom Kippur War ............................................................253, 265, 267

www.ingramcontent.com/pod-product-compliance
Lightning Source LLC
Chambersburg PA
CBHW071236160426
43196CB00009B/1083